MW00584082

PURGATORY

DANTE'S DIVINE TRILOGY PART 2
ENGLISHED IN PROSAIC VERSE
BY
ALASDAIR GRAY

CANONGATE BOOKS
EDINBURGH 2019

First published in Great Britain, the USA and Canada in 2019 by Canongate Books Ltd, 14 High Street, Edinburgh EH1 1TE

Distributed in the USA by Publishers Group West and in Canada by Publishers Group Canada

canongate.co.uk

1

The author gratefully acknowledges the support of Creative Scotland towards the publication of this book

British Library Cataloguing-in-Publication Data
A catalogue record for this book is available on request from the British Library

ISBN 978 1 78689 473 1

Typeset in Times New Roman by Biblichor Ltd, Edinburgh

Printed and bound in Great Britain by Clays Ltd, Elcograf S.p.A.

TRANSLATOR'S FOREWORD

Hell is underground, Heaven high above. Where on Earth is Purgatory? No heretics believed in it. Thomas Aquinas called it a fact human reason could not locate so should leave to God. Dante never feared imagining more than orthodox Catholics, and by combining their theology with Pagan science he placed Purgatory firmly where we place Australia.

Greeks and Romans had no evidence of land outside Europe, Asia and Africa, so thought a vast ocean covered the rest of the globe. Their geographers deduced that the polar regions furthest from the sun were too cold to support life, and the equator nearest the sun was too hot. Some wondered if the south temperate zone supported life but were sure this could never be known, as the equator would roast or boil explorers trying to cross. This meant Atlantic voyages could discover nothing good, so across the Strait of Gibraltar they imagined a sign: *THUS FAR AND NO FURTHER*. Dante decided this was a divine prohibition, because shortly before his time Italian merchants sought a faster way than overland to import Indian spices and Chinese silk. They sailed out past Gibraltar meaning to circumnavigate Africa and never returned.

This enforced Dante's Catholic cosmography. When God expelled the rebel angels (said theologians) they fell into an underground pit He had prepared for them. Dante described Hell as a conical space, the point at the centre of the world where Satan was stuck like a worm in a bad apple. Matter that formerly filled Hell's cavity had been expelled as an island-mountain in the south's ocean, exactly opposite Jerusalem in the north land mass. This was Purgatory, ringed by terraces with steep cliffs between, the lowest cliff surrounded by a coastal plain for new arrivals. Round the low cliff trudged sinful souls saved from Hell by last-minute repentances, but delayed from climbing to Heaven by excommunication. From a cave in that cliff Virgil led Dante after they ascended from Hell, as my cover design tries to show.

LIST OF

CANTOS

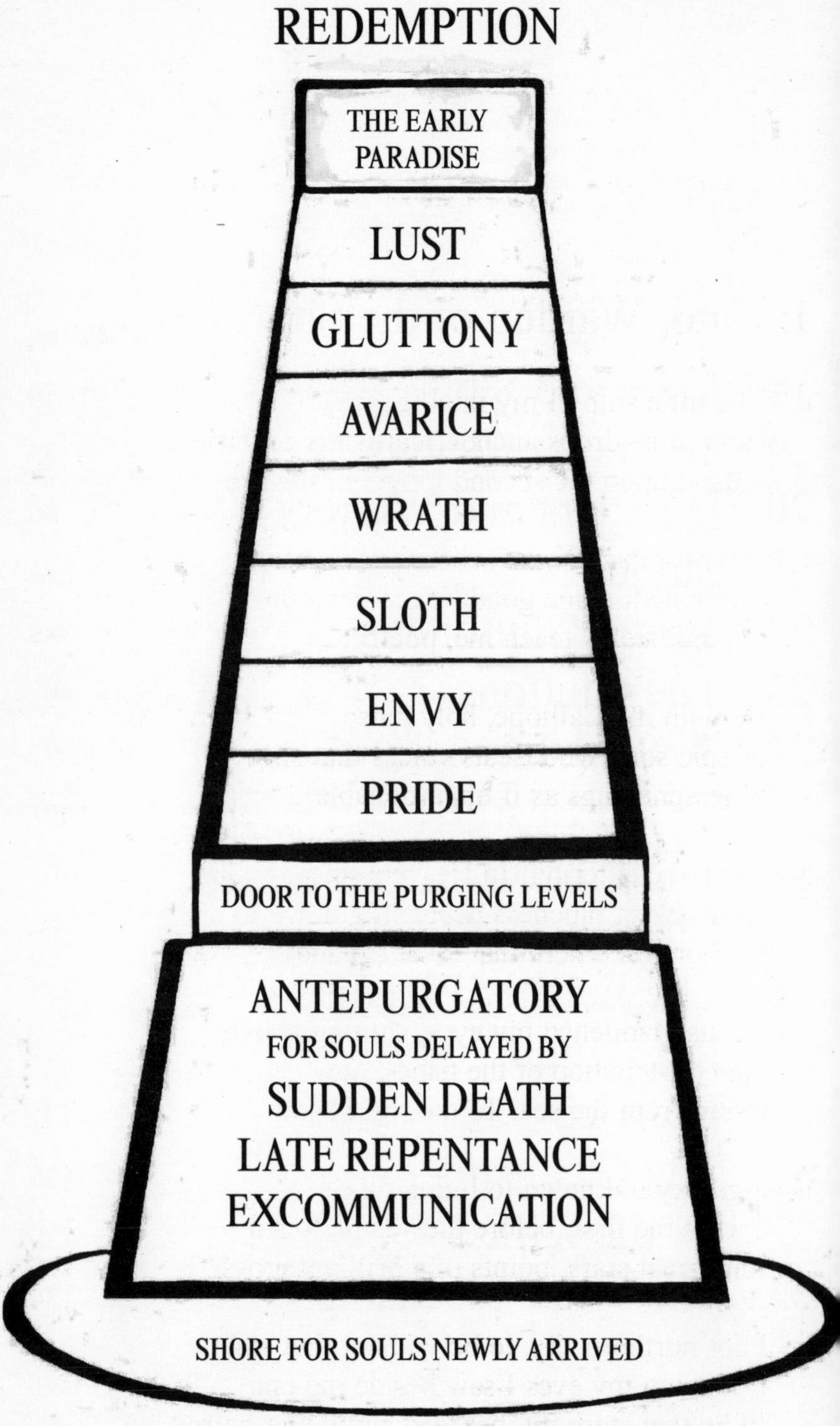

REDEMPTION

THE EARLY PARADISE

LUST

GLUTTONY

AVARICE

WRATH

SLOTH

ENVY

PRIDE

DOOR TO THE PURGING LEVELS

ANTEPURGATORY
FOR SOULS DELAYED BY
SUDDEN DEATH
LATE REPENTANCE
EXCOMMUNICATION

SHORE FOR SOULS NEWLY ARRIVED

PLAN OF MOUNT PURGATORY

1: Cato, Warden of the Shore

The little ship of my intelligence
furls sails, drops anchor, leaves the cruel sea.
I stand upon the second kingdom's beach

and now can sing of where each sinful soul
is purified, made good by reaching up
to paradise. O teach me, poetry!

Be with me Calliope, holy muse
of epic song who treats voices that sing
of lesser things as if unpardonable

magpie chattering! In Heaven's clear height
I saw sweet blueness deepening down to
the horizon where that lover's planet

Venus gladdened my eyes, shining above
the constellation of the fishes, now
rising from the sea. To the right I saw

a galaxy unknown to living folk
except the first, before they came to sin –
four great stars, points of a brilliant cross.

Poor northern sky, to be without that sight!
Dropping my eyes I saw beside me one
lit by that starlight, bearded and white-haired,

his face so full of venerable might
I wanted to adore him as his son.
"What are you," he demanded, "you that flee

eternal punishment? What guide, what lamp
lit your path out? Has Heaven changed its decree,
letting the damned souls free? Say by what right

you stand below my cliffs!" By word and hand
my guide made me bow knee and head then said,
"We have not come by our own will. Hear why.

When this man stood in peril of his soul
Heaven sent a lady, saying I should
lead him through Hell up to the highest good.

Now he has seen the deeps. May I show now
those sinners purified upon the steeps
where you preside? Be kind to him. He seeks

the liberty that you in Utica
perished to keep, shedding your coat of clay
to proudly wear it on the Judgement Day.

Our journey breaks no law. This man still lives.
Minos never judged him or me. I dwell
in the virtuous ring of Hell, close to

chaste Marcia, the wife who worships you.
For her sake let us climb the blessèd stairs
that lead to Heaven's grace. When I return

to Limbo she will hear how kind you are."
I saw this warden of the purging hill
was Cato, Caesar's foe, who stabbed himself

49 rather than see the Roman Empire kill
the glorious Republic that he loved.
Shaking his head he said, “Aye, Marcia

52 deserves all kindness, but since she has gone
beyond death’s river, Acheron, and I
stay here, why mention her? Since you obey

55 Heaven’s commands you need not use her name
for I obey them too. Lead him you guide
down to this island’s shore. Above the beach

58 in soft mud grow the reeds that never die.
Pluck one of these and tie it round his waist.
Wash his face first. Angels hate the sight

61 of grime from Hell. After, don’t come back here.
The rising sun will show a better place
to start your climb. Goodbye.” He disappeared.

64 I stood up when my leader said, “Dear child,
this plain slopes seaward. Let’s do as he told.”
A morning breeze fleeing before the dawn

67 came from the distant glitter of the sea.
We crossed that lonely plain like wanderers
seeking a path who fear they seek in vain.

70 The low sun’s level rays began to warm
the turf we trod, when my guide paused beside
a boulder’s shadow on a patch of grass

73 still misted with pearls of dew. I halted,
knowing what he would do. He stooped, wet hands,
washed my face clean of crusts left by fearful,

pitiful tears, restoring how I looked 76
before invading Hell. We reached the shore
no living foot had ever touched before.

Here, as instructed, Virgil plucked a reed, 79
and as he bound it round my waist I saw
a miracle, for where that rush once stood

sprang up another, just as tall and good. 82

2: Newcomers

1 By now the sun had left the northern sky
where at high noon it lights Jerusalem,
leaving the Ganges in the deepest night.

4 Seen from our shore the sky above the sea
took on a rosy glow, into which slid
that golden sphere of light. We stood and gazed

7 like wanderers who tarry on a road
before their journey starts. Then I beheld
beneath the sun, across the ocean floor

10 a sight I hope to see again – brightness
speeding so swiftly to us that no flight
of bird could equal it. When I gazed back

13 from questioning my master with a look,
it had grown brighter. On each side I saw
a whiteness I could not make out, above

16 something becoming clearer as it neared.
My master did not say a word until
the whitenesses appeared as wings, and then

19 seeing who moved that ship he cried, "Bend knees,
clasp hands, bow down before a cherubim
of God, for you will soon meet more of these.

See how without a sail or oar the ship
is driven by his Heaven-pointing wings –
by pure eternal plumes that never moult.”

The brightness of this dazzling bird of God
made me half close my eyes. He stood astern
of ship so light that the prow cleft no wave.

More than a hundred souls within it sat
singing King David’s psalm, *When Israel*
escaped from Egypt’s land, chanting *Amen*

on feeling that their vessel touched the strand.
The angel signed the cross over these souls
who sprang ashore. His ferry sped away

fast as it came. Passengers on the beach
stood looking round like strangers anywhere.
The sun had chased stars from the sky when one

approached and said, “Sirs, there is a mountain
we must climb. We do not know where to start,
can you show the way?” My guide said, “We two

are pilgrims just as ignorant as you,
come by a road so rough that further climb
to us will be child’s play.” A whisper grew

among these spirits that I lived and breathed.
They stared as if I were good news. One face
I knew, so ran to embrace that man. Alas,

my hands passed through his shade and hit my chest.
He smiled, withdrew. I cried, “Stay Casella –
I love you – tunes you gave my poems

make them popular! Why die before me?
And months ago! Why so long getting here?"
The sweet voice I knew said, "And I love you,

though gladly Heavenward bound. Remember
exactly thirteen centuries ago
Christ died for us. Our Pope proclaims this year

a Jubilee. All who hear mass in Rome
will have their sins forgiven. Hope of that
draws hoards of ancient dying pilgrims there.

The port for all not damned to Hell is where
Tiber joins the sea. Queues for that ferry
are very long these days, hence some delay

not troublesome to me. Heaven's decree
is best, but say why you stand *breathing* here!"
I said, "I live, so must return this way

when dead, like you, by the same ferry. Please,
if death has not deprived you of your art
sing verses I once wrote to cheer my heart."

He sang, *Love that converses with my mind*,
so sweetly that it sounds within me still.
My master and the others listened too,

as if it wholly occupied their will
till, like a thunderclap, Cato appeared
shouting, "You lazy louts, why linger here?

Run to the mountain! There strip off the sins
hiding your souls from God!" As pigeon flock
pecking the ground for seed, at sudden shock,

explodes into the air, these travellers 76
in panic fled that terrible old man
and spread across the plain, at the same time

racing blindly uphill, wholly unsure 79
what he or she was bound to find ahead.
Having no clue what better we could do

I and my leader were not far behind. 82

3: The Foothills

1 Our pace became more dignified upon
the foothills of that mount where climbing joins
goodness and reason. Since he had let me halt

4 to hear a song, Virgil had said no word.
His noble mind, believing no fault small,
suffered the sting of being in the wrong.

7 The rising sun shone rosy on our backs.
I gladly viewed the upward slope ahead
then felt it incomplete, for only one

10 shadow lay on the ground before my feet.
Afraid that suddenly I climbed alone
I gasped with dread. My comforter enquired,

13 "Why, even now, do you distrust my aid?
In Naples, underneath a monument
my shadow is entombed among my dust.

16 That I am shadowless is not more strange
than all the starry spheres of Heaven are.
Admiring wonder is the right response

19 to everything beyond your wisdom's range.
Thought alone *cannot* know the infinite
eternal Three-in-One creating all.

If human science could bring men to God
Mary need never have borne Jesus Christ,
or we in Limbo live unsatisfied

in outer Hell, far from the greatest good
where Homer, Plato, Aristotle dwell
with many more." He fell silent again,

staring with troubled face on ground we trod
until we reached Mount Purgatory's base.
The wildest mountainside in Italy

would look an easy staircase seen beside
this cliff too sheer, this granite precipice
too high and smooth for any mountaineer.

My master sighed and murmured, "Lacking wings,
we need to find a slope that legs can use.
It must exist. Do we turn left or right?"

He pondered where the ground met the rock wall.
I, looking round, saw, a sling-shot away,
a group of souls approaching from our left,

walking so slowly that at first I thought
they did not move at all. I shouted out,
"See Master! These may know where we should go."

He looked, then spoke with confidence renewed.
"Indeed they may, my son. Let us enquire
and never cease to hope." A thousand steps

brought us to where the flock of souls, like sheep,
walked timidly, heads bowed, behind a few
dignified leaders pacing slowly too.

49 "Hail, holy ones!" cried Virgil. "You have died
as Christians, so are sure of Heaven's grace.
Unlike you we must ascend at once. Please

52 where is the right place? Do you know of one?"
The leaders halted, stared and then drew back.
Their flock was scared and huddled to the rock.

55 My shadow on their track caused this dismay.
Virgil declared, "You need not feel surprise.
I will explain. My friend is still alive,

58 his body therefore splits the light of day.
Heaven demands we climb without delay.
Where can we do so?" "Turn and go with us,"

61 a leader of these good souls said. We did,
walked at a slow pace. "Perhaps," said one,
"you know my face?" I looked. He was fair-haired,

64 handsome, debonair, an eyebrow broken
by a scar. I admitted I did not,
whereupon, smiling, "Look at this," he said,

67 opening his vest to show in his chest
a much worse wound, adding "I am Manfred,
ruler of Sicily, Tory warlord

70 who defied the Pope, so died by the sword.
As my blood flowed I gave my soul with tears
to Him who saves all sinners who repent,

73 even of crimes as horrible as mine.
The victors built a cairn over my bones.
He that comes to me I will not cast out,

Christ said that but Pope Clement disagreed, 76
had the cairn broken, bones scattered around,
on unholy ground battered by wind and rain.

We in this troop though excommunicate, 79
will be redeemed at last, though for each year
unconfessed souls normally wait to climb

the purifying stair to Heaven's gate, 82
we under papal ban wait thirty more.
That time can be reduced by living souls.

I beg you please when back on Earth again, 85
tell my daughter Constance, Aragon's queen,
mother of kings, to pray well for my soul.

Despite Pope Clement I am not in Hell." 88

4: The First Ascent

1 Pleasure or pain can fill us up so full
they dominate all ways we think and act,
a fact disproving Plato's rule that souls

4 are triple – vegetable, animal
and logical. Words can so occupy
our soul, we do not notice passing time.

7 Manfred so pleased me that I did not see
the sun rise to its fiftieth degree.
Mid-morning passed before our company

10 aroused me, crying, "Here's the place you need!"
I saw in the cliff face a gap as wide
as in a vineyard hedge that peasants block

13 with a forkful of thorn, yet wide enough
to admit a man into a deep crack
sloping steeply up. My guide, stepping in,

16 started climbing on all fours, rock beneath,
beside and above his back. I followed,
bidding the slowly moving flock goodbye.

19 You may rush down Noli, up San Leo,
mount Bismantova's summit on your feet.
Urgent desire drove fast my hands and knees.

I scrambled after Virgil, did not stop 22
until we reached the precipice's top
and stood upon the edge of a broad ledge

of that bare mountainside. "Master," said I, 25
"where now?" "Upward," said he, "and do not halt
before you meet a wiser guide than me."

He turned to lead me up a steeper slope 28
than we had tackled in the creviced rock.
Exhausted I cried, "Pause kind father, please!

You're leaving me behind – I need to rest!" 31
"My son," said he, pointing not far ahead,
"drag yourself first up there." I forced my feet

to follow him up to a level ground, 34
a terrace curving round the mighty hill,
and sat facing the way we came (often

the finest view) due east. First I gazed down, 37
feasting eyes on the sea below, then raised
them to the skies, amazed to see the sun

shining upon my left. "How can this be?" 40
I said. "This island mountain," he replied,
"is central to the southern hemisphere,

just as the land where Christ was crucified 43
is central to the north. Halfway between
lies the equator. When the setting sun

crossed that, it left the north in night and brought 46
light here, to the western point, which is not
upon your right, but on the other hand.

Do you understand?" I did, then asked him,
"Have we much more to climb? The height ahead
is out of sight." He said, "The hardest part

of leaving sin is always at the start.
The climb is easier as you go up.
Near the top you will feel climbing is like

floating downstream in a boat." A voice said,
"You'll sit down pretty often before that."
We turned and saw a rock within whose shade

folk squatted, looking totally fatigued.
The speaker hugged his knees, head sunk between.
I told my guide, "That is Belacqua, sir –

a Florentine well-known for being slow."
Belacqua raised an eye above his thigh
and grunted, "Busybody, up you go

now you know why the sun shines on your left."
Smiling a bit at that I said to him,
"You need not grumble friend. You're safe from Hell

but why sit here? What are you waiting for?
Have you not shaken off your laziness?"
"Brother," he groaned, "I cannot go up yet,

I died too soon to properly confess
my life of sinful sloth before my death.
The angel-warden of the higher gate

cannot admit me up to cleansing pain
until I've squatted here for sixty years –
the years before I gave my soul to God.

No living souls will pray to lessen these 76
and my despair. O how I envy you!"
Virgil, climbing ahead, called back to me,

"Time to go on!" I left Belacqua there. 79

5: The Unconfessed

1 I left these ghosts to follow him uphill,
and then heard other voices shouting, “Look!
Sunlight won’t pierce him, so he is not dead!”

4 Turning my head I saw an eager crowd
staring upon my shadow and at me.
“Words should not turn you – face the uphill track,”

7 my leader cried. “Good heads should imitate
strong towers undisturbed by windy blast.
Ignore what people say. Distracted minds

10 go easily astray because each thought
cancels the last.” “Coming!” I called (for what
else could I say?) and blushing with shame,

13 climbed up to him. From round the hill above
penitents came, chanting King David’s psalm,
The Miserere, grieving for past sin.

16 At sight of me their chant became an “Oo!”
and two ran down to us, crying, “Please say,
what kind of man are you?” My guide replied,

19 “Tell your folk that he (as his shadow proves)
is flesh and blood, able to do them good
if they respect him as they should.” No cloud

soared swifter through the sky than they returned
to that crowd who, hearing their news, then wheeled
round like a troop of cavalry and then

came charging down. My guide said, "Know that these
will beg you to take word of them to Earth,
but don't stop climbing. Listen as you go."

"O lucky soul, ascending to delight,"
one cried. "On legs your mother made, please
look at us hard. Do you see any here

whose names you could take back to those we love?
They do not know the manner of our deaths,
deaths so obscure that we could not confess

but are not damned to Hell. A final pang of grief
for our past sins admitted Heaven's Grace,
which brought us here where prayers from pure hearts

can make us fit to see God's face, and these
are now our agonising need." I said,
"I see none here I know. Tell me your names,

if that will ease your pains and speed your climb
if it does not halt mine. I must obey
one who forbids delay while leading me

from world to world, but truly I declare,
by peace we all desire, to do my best."
"No need to swear – we trust your kindly words,"

their spokesman said. "I will first give my name:
Jacopo Cassero, Fano my town
between Naples ruled by Charles of Anjou

49 and states claimed by the Pope. Please visit there.
Ask people to say orisons that will
help shed the sorry burden of my guilt.

52 The Marquis of Ferrara spilt my blood
in secret, just to gratify his wrath.
At Oriaco near to Padua

55 (that traitor's town) his men ambushed my path.
Stabbed and confused I fled quite the wrong way
into the marsh, stumbled through mud and reeds,

58 fell bleeding, and saw my heart's blood at last
stain a pool red." Another spoke to me,
"May you meet what you seek upon this hill,

61 then back on Earth find some who'll pray for me.
I am from Montefeltro, once its count,
foxy old Guido's son, but few there now

64 care for me. My widow Joan does not,
and so you find me here with troubled brow."
Surprised, I cried, "But you and I once fought

67 at Campoldino! Afterwards I heard
your corpse was missing. None knew where it went.
Was that through malice or by accident?"

70 He said, "A demon drowned my solid part
after my soul was saved. I will explain.
I left that fight unhorsed and with slashed throat,

73 my blood dabbling the plain until I reached
a stream called Archiano that flows down
into the Arno from the Apennines.

Falling upon its bank I lost my sight
praying to God, and died with Mary's name
on my wicked lips. Let the living know

what happened then. God's angel took my soul.
The fiend from Satan yelled, "I have been robbed!
You carry off this man's eternal part

all for one tiny tear! See what I do
to his remains!" With wind and mist he swelled
clouds over the plain from Protomagno

to the mountain range, then burst them into
more torrential rain than earth could contain,
flooding to overflow gully and stream.

Bursting Archiano's banks, they swept my corpse
into the Arno, breaking it apart.
The bits were sunk in mud." A third shade said,

"When back on Earth and rested from your climb
tell people of La Pia. My birthplace
was Sienna. Maremma saw my death

as he knows well, the man who wedded me."

6: Of Italian States

1 Gamblers breaking the bank are thronged upon
by some who hope good luck rubs off on them,
and others wanting shares in what they gain.

4 Souls pressed on me like that, so very thick
I waved my hands in air to drive them back,
promising all these violently slain

7 to do the best I could. First, the good judge
stabbed in court by that man of blood, Tacco;
Guccio who, fleeing Campoldino,

10 was swallowed too by Arno's stormy flood;
the Pisan who forgave the enemies
who slew his son; Frederick Novello;

13 Count Orso; Peter Brosse wrongly hanged
by the Queen of Brabant. (Let her beware
of joining ugly company in Hell.)

16 When free of these and others begging me
to tell their kindred they needed prayers
I begged my guide, "Master, enlighten me.

19 Your *Aeneid* says that divine decree
cannot be altered by the human will.
Surely that means these beg my help in vain?"

"I wrote plain truth," said he, "but wrote before 22
God came in mercy to humanity,
was born as a divinely honest man

who suffered and defeated wretched death. 25
Since then, when justice is embraced by love
in a last moment of pure penitence,

justice and mercy form one healing flame. 28
Be patient if you do not understand.
Enlightenment awaits you high above,

smiling in bliss. Her name is Beatrice." 31
I shouted, "Master, let us hurry up!
I am not tired now, and before sun sets

will climb up very fast to reach the top." 34
"Before that Heavenly event," said he,
"the sun will set twice more, but just ahead

sits one who may know an easier ascent." 37
Him we approached was Lombard. With calm pride
he gazed on us as resting lions do

out of moving eyes. When Virgil asked 40
where lay the way up he did not say,
but asked from where we came. My leader said,

"Mantua," at which the soul, leaping up, 43
embraced him, cried, "My city! Know that I,
Sordello, am poet of Mantua,

only excelled by one born long ago." 46
Then Virgil happily embraced him too.
O Italy, you hostelry of slaves!

49 You vessel, captainless in stormy sea!
Why cannot souls who love their cities well
co-operate to keep their country whole?

52 Even within a single city wall
new money fights with old, each wrestling for
a strangle-hold, making alliances

55 with foreigners through bribery, bad pacts
which are not kept, preventing unity.
There is no peace within Italian shores.

58 Unlike beehives who recognise a queen
you are a brothel, ruled by squabbling whores.
The Emperor Justinian once made

61 a legal code to pacify his land
which other lands employ – not Italy,
which won't submit to legal spurs and bit.

64 None is allowed to take the reins in hand.
Devout priests should obey our Lord's command
and let a Caesar ride our Latin steed.

67 O German Albert, Holy Roman King,
all Europe should be yours, but you don't heed
its central garden which has run to seed.

70 Come, govern us! Our wretched noblemen,
Montagues, Capulets, Filippeschi,
Monaldi dread each other! Unite us

73 under one head we all should recognise!
Rome, a poor widow, weeps for your great work
of restoration. Pity and help Rome

become the Queen of Christendom again 76
or pity your reputation. And may
almighty Jove, once crucified for us,

not turn away from our chaotic state. 79
Tyrants dominate Italian towns
where mob-rule is not led by rascal clowns.

My Florence, this digression won't touch you 82
where citizens take public good to heart
and to their tongue. You are too smart for rule

by mob or tyrant. Athens and Sparta 85
did not legislate constantly like you.
Elsewhere folk dodge the burdens of the state –

your people grab for office before asked, 88
and so are peaceful, rich – except when not!
You change your constitution in a week,

laws, government and coinage restlessly, 91
improving nothing like a sick woman
tossing and turning in her bed and sure

each new position may achieve a cure. 94

7: The Climb Halts

1 Those Mantuans, Sordello and my guide,
embraced each other happily until
the first drew back enquiring, “Who are you?”

4 “A soul from Hell,” the greater poet said.
“Augustus, the first Emperor of Rome,
buried my bones before the Christian faith

7 let saved souls make a staircase of this hill,
so I, Virgil, will not reach paradise.”
Like one who thinks, “This is . . . it cannot be!

10 It must . . . but surely not?” Sordello stood
wondering, as if his eyes perceived
a marvel far too great to be believed,

13 then bowed as low as anybody could.
“You are the glory of the Latin race!”
he cried, “Through you our language is as strong,

16 will live as long, as Gospel scriptures do.
Tell me the miracle that brings you here,
and if you think me fit to know, from which

19 cloister of Hell.” Said Virgil, “I have come
through all the rings of Hell, but dwell with souls
who do not suffer pain. Ours is the state

of babies who die before christening
cleans off their sinful stain. We do not weep
but sigh for what we, living, could not know

so cannot now enjoy eternally –
true faith, hope, charity. But even so
Heaven has ordered me to lead this man

up to the mountain's height. Since sunset casts
its shadow on us we will climb by night,
having not reached real Purgatory yet.

Sordello, can you tell us the right way?"
"Yes, I will be your guide a while," said he,
"but not uphill at once. Now you must halt

and be escorted to a resting place
where you will find folk you'll be glad to see."
"Why? Who bans our divinely ordered climb?"

my master cried, "Do you?" Sordello stooped,
drew a line with his finger on the ground,
and said, "When light departs you won't cross this.

None forbids night climbing here, but darkness
abolishes all wish to climb, though letting
any drift backward down the way they came."

My master brooded, then said, "Lead us please
to where you say a rest will do us good."
He led us in the gloaming a short way

toward a corrie hollowing the slope,
then said, "Here we will wait for a new day
deep in the mountain's lap." A winding path

that rose and fell brought us to that deep dell.
We stood upon the edge where, gazing down
there still was light enough to see below

a glowing lawn as green as emerald
with blossoms golden, crimson, pearly white,
silver and azure and pure indigo.

All colours of the rainbow were surpassed
by blooms feasting our eyes. Their fragrances
blent in one sweetness, lovely but unknown

to living men before I breathed that air,
and there sat souls unseen by lower folk
singing the Holy Hymn to Heaven's Queen.

"Before the sun now setting leaves the sky,"
Sordello said, "we need descend no more.
Why? Those below are clearly seen from here.

He who sits highest of that kingly crew,
too glum to move his lips in sacred song
was Rudolph, Emperor, who failed to heal

wounds that have mangled Italy so long.
Trying to comfort him is Ottocar,
King of Bohemia, in his nappies

better than bearded Wenceslaus, his son
who lazily now occupies his throne.
That snub-nosed chap beating his breast in grief

regrets how he disgraced the Crown of France.
That vicious thief, his son, has gone to Hell
but see *his* daughter's husband, formerly

the Prince of Anjou, also torn by grief. 76
You see two monarchs sing in harmony –
stout Tory King of Aragon beside

the manly-nosed Whig King of Sicily. 79
Their sons have none of their nobility.
How seldom vigour in a parent tree

enters its branches! Only God knows why. 82
See England's Henry sit apart, alone,
a simple king whose Edward, Prince of Wales,

is now a hammer of the French and Scots. 85
Lowest and looking up, unluckiest
prince of this age, William of Montferrat

who, tricked by foes, died in an iron cage." 88

8: The Vestibule

When church bells toll the knell of parting day
the traveller, whether on land or sea
remembers home and loved ones far away.

While pondering Sordello's final word
I saw a kingly soul below arise,
showing by gestures that he would be heard.

Joining his palms he lifted them in prayer,
and gazing to the east, began to sing
sweetly the evening hymn to Heavenly light.

The rest melodiously joined the hymn
while also gazing on the bright clear stars
which were, I noticed, starting to appear.

Reader, sharpen your mind's eye to the truth
I try to show you through my poem's veil
which should be thinnest, most transparent here.

The noble company fell silent, all
looking up humbly and expectantly,
to where I saw descending through the air

a pair of angels holding shining swords
shortened because their points were broken off.
Their wings and robes were green as fresh spring leaves.

One stopped above our heads, the other stood
upon the mountainside just opposite.
Though I could clearly see their flaxen hair,

the brightness of their eyes quite dazzled me.
Sordello said, “Mary, Mother of God,
sends them to guard the valley at this time

from the foul snake, our spiteful enemy.”
Unsure of where that snake would come, I pressed
against the trusty shoulder of my guide.

“We will descend and greet some noble shades,”
Sordello said, “for speech with you will please
that company.” By three steps I went down

to where I saw (though air was darkening)
a man whose face I knew, as he knew mine –
noble judge Nino. That he was not damned

delighted me. “When did you land upon
this island’s shore?” he asked. “At dawn today,”
I said, “although I did not cross the sea.

I am not dead, but came on foot through Hell.”
He started back, then said to someone near,
“Conrad, arise! See what God’s grace has willed.”

Then said to me, “By that great gratitude
you owe to Him whose deepest purposes
cannot be known, when back in Italy,

beg my child Joan to pray God for my soul.
He will respond to prayers of innocence.
My wife, who wed again, loves me no more,

49 showing how soon the flame of women's love
dies lacking sight and touch to kindle it.
She cannot long enjoy her present mate.

52 Her husband flaunts a viper on his shield.
Carved on her tomb it will not look as fair
as would the chanticleer she had from me."

55 The indignation showing in his face
came from the heart, but I was staring up
to that high centre where stars move most slow.

58 My leader asked, "What are you seeing there?"
"Three starry torches new to me," said I,
"with which the southern sky is all aglow."

61 Said he, "The four great stars you saw at dawn
have sunk from view and are replaced by these."
And it was then Sordello cried aloud,

64 "See! There's the enemy!" pointing to where
the valley's side dipped low, for there a snake
was sliding in, maybe that subtle one

67 who first had given bitter food to Eve.
Through grass and flowers it undulated on,
an evil streak, twisting at times its neck

70 to lick its back with flickering forked tongue.
So swiftly did Heaven's hawks swoop down at him
I only heard their green wings cleave the air

73 before that serpent fled and they returned.
He whom the judge had called to look at me
had not since looked away. Approaching now

he said, “May your will to ascend this hill 76
not fail before you reach the greatest height.
If you have word of Val di Magra or

places near by, then tell it to me please 79
for there I once was great, known by the name
my father had, Conrad Malaspina.

My too much loving of my family 82
here must be purified.” “I was never
in your land,” I replied, “but in Europe

where are you not renowned? Guilty tongues fail 85
to slander your name, for it still resounds
for generosity of purse and sword –

a family famous for going straight.” 88
He said, “Years hence I happily foresee
experience will prove your friendly view

of my folk’s generosity still true.” 91

9: The Entrance

Upon the little valley's verdant floor
I, Virgil, Sordello, Nino the judge
and Conrad Malespina spoke no more

and I, imperfect man, slept deep until
that early hour when swallows, sensing dawn,
mournfully cheep and sleepers, not disturbed

by dreams of bodily and mental stress
sometimes see visions of pure blessèdness.
A golden-feathered eagle seemed to be

hovering overhead with wings outspread.
I thought, "That bird seized Ganymede to be
butler in Paradise, so fair was he.

He won't want me!" Then like a thunderbolt
it swooped and, snatching, soared with me up, up,
up to the height of Empyrean fire

where the imagined heat fused us in one
before at last (of course) awaking me.
The mother of Achilles carried him

asleep from Crete to a Greek island where
his opening eyes knew nothing he could see.
Two hours after day dawned I woke like that,

cold, weak, and staring at the ocean's shore
far, far below. My comforter and guide
seated at my side said, "Do not be afraid.

Your state is excellent. Before day broke,
as you were fast asleep upon the flowers
that clothe the lower dell, a lady came.

She said, *I, Lucy, come to lift this man*
and take him, sleeping, further on his way.
Sordello stayed with other noble souls

as when this clear day dawned she took you up,
I following until she laid you here
and pointed to that gate before she left."

Made confident once more I rose to face
the rampart of the mountainside, my guide
leading me up to a much higher place

than we had been before. Reader, please know
I must rise to a higher theme, sustained
by greater art. We reached what at first seemed

a cleft in that rock wall, but was a gate
above three coloured steps, each different.
On the threshold a silent warder sat,

his face so bright I could not bear the sight,
and in his hand he held a naked sword
I also could not look on steadily,

for it reflected light so dazzlingly.
"Where are you from? What do you seek?" he said.
"If no Heavenly escort brings you here,

49 beware! This upward climb may do you harm."
"A messenger from Heaven," said my guide,
"recently pointed us toward this gate.

52 Her name was Lucy." "Enter then, and climb,"
the courteous warder said, so I set foot
on a white marble slab so polished smooth

55 it mirrored me exactly as I am.
The second step was purple, rough and cracked
throughout its length and breadth. The topmost step

58 resembled porphyry, as red as blood
spurted from vein. The angel's feet reposed
on this. The threshold where he sat above

61 was clearly of the hardest adamant.
On these three steps my leader led me up,
saying, "Now ask him to fling wide the gate."

64 I threw myself down at his holy feet,
and after beating on my breast three times
begged him to mercifully let me through.

67 With his sword point he etched upon my brow
seven Ps, then said, "As you climb within
these will be healed away." Out of his robe

70 of ashen colour he removed two keys,
one gold, one silver. Turning in the lock
the white first, then the yellow, he explained,

73 "When both keys do not turn the gate stays shut.
One is more precious but the other needs
more skill, more wisdom, to make it unlock.

Peter who gave them told me if I erred 76
to err on mercy's side, so in you come
but don't look back or you will be expelled."

When Caesar burst in through a temple door 79
to rob Tarpeian gold, they thundered loud.
The hinges here roared louder grinding round,

but entering I heard sweet voices sound 82
blending with organ chords, and ringing clear
in the *Te Deum*, mighty mirthful hymn,

which most of all on Earth I love to hear. 85

10: The First Terrace

1 And so the angel warder let us through
that gate locked fast to those of evil will.
We climbed a narrow track in the cleft hill,

4 nor did I dare look round when at my back
the gate shut with a clang that shook the ground.
Our steep path zig-zagged sharply left and right.

7 Said Virgil, "This will test your climbing skill,
so concentrate." I did. It was near noon
when I emerged from that tight needle's eye.

10 Footsore and tired I stood beside my guide,
like him, unsure of where to go again:
sheer drop behind, on each side empty plain,

13 ahead a sheer cliff three men's height away.
We had not moved a step before I knew
the cliff we faced was marble, pure and white,

16 splendidly carved with shapes so well devised
they could not be the work of human hands
and recognised just One could make them so.

19 We saw the angel Gabriel announce
the birth of Jesus Christ, the Prince of Peace
for whom mankind has wept through centuries.

He seemed to say, *Hail Mary, full of grace!*
and the humility of her reply,
Here am I, God's servant, glowed in her face

so I believed I heard her with my ears.
"Look over here," my guide said, pointing to
images of a more crowded scene:

oxen pulling a cart holding the ark
brought by King David to Jerusalem.
Seven jubilant choirs surrounded it.

My eyes declared, "They sing!" my ears, "They don't!"
and where, in marble, clouds of incense rose,
eyes disagreed with nose. Before the ark,

the psalmist monarch with his robe tucked up
danced like a happy clown. His wife looked down
from a high window, smiling scornfully

at his humiliating lack of pride.
Beside this was another crowded scene:
Emperor Trajan riding forth to war

with knights and retinue. Eagles above
flapped golden wings. A poor widow clung
to his bridle, cried, "Sir, my murdered son

should be avenged!" "He will be, when I return."
"But if you don't?" "My heir will do what's right."
"If you don't do what's needed now," cried she,

"then why should he?" "True!" Trajan said, halting,
"none should delay just acts." Justice was done.
Our best Pope since Saint Peter, Gregory,

49 esteemed this just humility as proof
of Trajan's noble Christianity,
so he is now redeemed in Paradise.

52 These splendid visions of true humbleness
pleased me by showing truth and beauty one
till I heard Virgil murmur, "Here come they

55 who should point out the stair to the next heights."
I looked to see some kind of cavalcade,
then said, "There are no people in my sight!

58 Here's a slow avalanche of heavy stones
advancing on the ground. Sir, please explain."
Said he, "Stoop down and look. Under those weights

61 see once proud sinners crawling on their knees."
I cried out, "O you poor ones who believed
that wealth and power could magnify your worth!

64 Now crushed to earth, at last you will discard
your pride, a grubby caterpillar shell
splitting to loose angelic butterfly,

67 soaring to God upon His Judgement Day."
I quite forgot I might be one of them.
Brackets supporting ceilings on high walls

70 are sometimes carved like men, knees squeezed to chest.
Those here were just like that, sorely oppressed,
and the most patient ghosts were weeping most.

73 Their state was nearly more than they could bear.

11: The Proud

Our Father in Heaven, unlimited
except by your great love for all you made,
and everything you've given us on Earth,

we praise your name as angels do above.
Teach us to find your House of Peace on high
which by our strength alone we cannot reach

however hard and painfully we try.
Give everyone the nourishment we need
to rightly follow in the steps of Christ

and not slide backwards into sinful ways.
Forgive our sins as we also forgive
those who have hurt us. Dear Lord, most of all

do not let enemies become so strong
they drive the virtuous to doing wrong.
Lord God, you know that prayer is not for us,

but souls alive whose state is not redeemed.
Thus those ghosts prayed for us while toiling on
beneath such weight as we have never dreamed.

Let we with any goodness pray that they
are quicker lightened, raised above the moon
to their appointed place in Paradise.

22 Reading my mind I heard kind Virgil say,
"May all who stoop here be unburdened soon
and wing their upward flight. I lead a man

25 still clad in Adam's flesh, so we need stairs
to climb this cliff. Can any of you say
if nearest way is to our left or right?"

28 We could not see who spoke, but heard a voice.
"Go with us to the right, where there's a place
a man may climb. Were I not bent so low

31 I might see a face, recognise a friend
who pitied me. I was Italian,
my dad the great Bill Aldobrandesco –

34 Surely you know his name? Pride in my birth
and famous ancestors made me forget
all of us share one common mother, Earth.

37 Arrogance killed me, dragged to infamy
my name and kin. In Campagnatico
children know this and in Sienna too.

40 I am Umberto, whose excessive pride
will crush me until God is satisfied."
To hear him I'd bent low and so saw one

43 who did not speak but twisted round his neck
to see me, knew me, kept his eyes on me
as he crept onward very painfully.

46 Bent almost double at his side I cried,
"You, Oderisi! Pride of Gubbio
for illustrating books, or (as they say

in Paris) for illuminating them."
"Brother," said he, "Franco of Bologna
does that much better now. His claim to fame

is partly due to what he learned from me.
When living I denied how good he was.
Here I am purging all that pettiness.

The emptiness of glory in a name
is obvious. Florence once gloried in
the radiance of Cimabue's art.

Giotto's fame has cast a shade on it.
Guido Guinizelli's verse was once
the splendour of our tongue. Cavalcanti's

is now more highly sung. Who's next? Are you?
Who cares? A thousand years, two thousand, ten,
are eye-blinks to the slowly turning spheres

of Paradise. Fame is a brief noise.
He crawling before me once had a name
shouted through Tuscany, and adored

in Sienna, where it's now ignored, though
he helped it smash a mad Florentine horde."
"Your true words humble me, but tell me more,"

I said, "about that lord who crawls before."
"He, Provenzan Salvani, tried to be
Sienna's tyrant prince and so creeps thus

like all of us who raised ourselves far too
presumptuously high." Said I, "But why,
is he not below with other princes

76 not yet fit for your purifying pain?"
Oderisi said, "He earned this higher place
because once, when a despot but not rich,

79 he begged for money in the public square
to ransom a dear friend, though his proud soul
found this humiliation agony.

82 You too will know the pain of beggary."

12: Going from Pride

Like two slow oxen harnessed in one yoke
I, bending almost double at his side,
crept onward till my gentle master spoke:

"Leave him; we must go faster now." I did,
though inwardly depressed, but very soon
followed my leader eagerly. We seemed

lighter of foot. Said he, "Start looking down.
There's splendid entertainment where we tread."
As flat stones in a graveyard often show

carvings provoking memories and tears,
each vivid surface of the mountain street
was paved with wonders of mosaic art,

all showing penalties of too much pride.
I saw the noblest creature God first made
falling like lightning. On the other side

I saw the fifty-headed, hundred-armed
Briareus dismembered by Jove's dart;
I saw Jove's armoured children as they viewed

the scattered limbs – Apollo, Pallas, Mars;
I saw King Nimrod, Babel's architect
bewildered, staring at his futile heap;

and poor Niobe, statue who bled tears
with seven sons and seven daughters dead;
and Saul, the conquered King of Israel,

on Gilboa self-slaughtered by his sword;
and mad Arachne, half a spider now,
still clinging to the woeful web she wove;

and Rehoboam, boastful coward king,
fleeing by chariot, though none pursued.
That pavement also showed me how and why

Alcmaeon slew his mother, who betrayed
his father for a jewelled ornament;
Assyria's great king Sennacherib,

stabbed in a temple by his ruthless sons,
afloat in a big cup of his own blood;
Cyrus's head, popped by Queen Tomyris

who said, "You liked bloodshed? So drink up this."
It showed Assyrians in panic flight
when General Holofernes lost *his* head;

and lastly saw the broken walls and ash
of mighty Troy, brought pitifully low.
No human artist could contrive to show

these histories in carving or in paint
so wonderfully well. The dead looked dead,
the living seemed to breathe. I came to see

the fate of pride spelled on that road for me,
but go your haughty ways, great sons of Eve!
Do not believe what's written on the ground.

I had not seen how far we and the sun
had circled round the hill when Virgil said,
"The time for brooding's past. Look upward – see,

the hour is noon. An angel's coming fast
who will direct us to the upward way,
so give him all the reverence he's due.

Today, you know, will never dawn again."
Knowing my master hated waste of time
I followed him in haste. We came to halt

before a lovely creature clad in white
whose face gleamed on us like the morning star.
Spreading his arms to us and then his wings,

he, pointing to a deep cleft in the cliff,
told us, "Climb here! It is an easy way.
Why do so few arrive to share it now?

Mankind was made to soar. What little flaws
detain the multitudes so far below?
But up you go." His wings then brushed my brow.

The cloven rock contained a noble stair
like that arising from the Arno bridge
(built when my city had just government)

rising to where all Florence can be viewed,
before the church of Miniato's door.
Then as we climbed I heard a sweeter voice

than words can tell, sing *Blessèd are the meek*,
unlike the lamentable screams I heard
between one level and the next in Hell.

76 I found that climbing up that holy stair
was easier than walking on flat ground.
"Master," I asked, "what weight has been removed?"

79 "The weight of that first P and what it means,
rubbed from your brow by the angelic wings,"
said he. "The rest are there more faintly now.

82 All will be cancelled, one by one, until
your body is so lightened by good will,
you'll not be capable of weariness."

85 Then I behaved like all those unaware
of how they look before the stares of folk
begin to worry them: they use their hands

88 to feel what they can't see and don't yet know.
With five spread fingertips I felt my head
and found six Ps where seven were before.

91 My guide smiled as he saw me doing so.

13: The Envious

We reached the summit of the stair and stood
upon the second terrace of the hill
that heals its climbers. Here another road

was winding by a steeper curve, a road
empty of people, shadow, ornament,
and colour: just dull stone. The poet said,

"Waiting to ask the way will cause delay,"
and turning right to face the sun he cried,
"Sweet light of day I choose you as our guide,

until it's obvious we've gone astray."
We strode so briskly to the right that soon
a mile was passed, and then toward us came

clear sentences, spoken by none we saw
who sounded kind. "They have no wine" came first,
flew by us, went repeating on behind,

fading, but not quite lost in distance when
"I am Orestes" followed it, and then
while I said, "Father, what do these words mean?"

a third voice came: "Love those who injure you."
My kind guide said, "Envy is cut back here
by whips of love, which are its opposite.

22 More sounds like these will strike your ear, I think,
before you leave this street, but look ahead.
See, at the cliff-foot many people sit."

25 I, staring forward harder, could detect
in robes coloured like stone on which they leaned
a mournful row, and nearer heard them groan:

28 "Pray for us, Mary", "Peter", "All the saints",
I do not think there walks on Earth today
any so hard that pity would not pierce

31 at sight of those I saw in so much pain.
Each, wearing coarse grey hair-cloth, lay with head
propped on a neighbour's shoulder like the blind

34 paupers who beg beside confessionals.
Tight iron wires stitched their eyelids shut.
Ashamed to see and not be seen I turned

37 toward my counsellor and he advised,
"Yes, question these, but use the fewest words."
He stood beside the road's perilous edge

40 which had no parapet, facing the shades,
whose cheeks were wet with tears squeezed sorely through
their eyelids' horrid seam. I turned to them

43 and said, "You who are sure to see one day
when consciousness and memory run clean,
are there among you some Italian souls?

46 It may be good for such a one or two
if I speak for you on the Earth below."
"O brother, all of us are citizens

of one great city. All Italians
are pilgrims to it, and not only they."
These words came from a little further on.

I moved to where a small expectant face
was tilted up. "Spirit, if it was you,"
I said, "who spoke, make yourself known by place

or else by name." "Sienna was my town,"
said she, "and here I mourn my sinful life
weeping to Him who gave Himself for us.

Named Sapia, although not sapient,
failure in others more delighted me
than my good luck. I was an old woman

when Sienna's Tories fought Florentine Whigs.
Seeing the faction that I hate retreat
with mad delight I loudly swore to God,

Now I don't fear you! as the blackbird sings
at sight of briefest sunlight in the spring.
This blasphemy will be forgiven since

Peter (a saint who lived by selling combs)
in charity both grieved and prayed for me.
But who are you who ask about my state?

You have I think, wide eyes and talk with breath."
I said, "My eyes will not be here for long.
Envy has never been my greatest sin.

My fear is of the punishment for pride –
I dread that crushing misery below,
but let me know what I can do for you

when I return to Earth." "How strange," said she.
"God loves you, letting you go up and down.
Please pray for me sometimes, and tell my kin

if you pass through Sienna, I am here.
They invest in schemes to renew old streams
and at Talamone build a new port

by trading oversea. Alas, the cost
will be private and public bankruptcy.
My family's great fortune will be lost,

and hopeful admirals will lose the most."

14: Of Envious Rulers

"Who now ascends our penitential hill 1
before death makes him rise, and who at will
opens and shuts his eyes?" "I do not know

but he is nearest you. Speak well to him, 4
to gain a fair reply." We saw two souls
conversing thus in that blind row. One said,

"O living man bound Heavenward, please tell 7
in charity your birthplace and your name.
A special grace protects you, so your words

can do us good." "I was born near," said I, 10
"a stream that flows more than a hundred miles
from Falterona to the sea. My name

you do not need. It's not yet known to fame." 13
"Mount Falterona is the source," said he
"of Tiber and of Arno, therefore you

are from Romagna or from Tuscany, 16
and probably the last. Why not say so?
Is Arno a bad word?" "It is indeed!"

the other speaker cried, "All living by 19
that evil flood should die and be forgot.
They flee from virtue, dread it like a snake.

22 The place corrupts them, or bad custom spreads
corruption through them like a deadly plague.
Close to the Arno's source the folk are brutes

25 like those whom Circe once turned into swine,
fit to eat acorns, not to dine like men.
Leaving these hogs the stream enters a land

28 of snarling mongrel dogs, more full of spite
than bravery or any strength to bite.
Lower the stream swells wider, and as

31 it swells, the dogs become rapacious wolves.
Leaving them by a winding glen it flows
through land of cheating foxes none can trap,

34 so great is the support for their deceit.
But now the future has grown clear to me!
I'll say what I foresee, and do not care

37 what ears may hear. Your grandson will become
hunter of wolves beside that horrid flood,
selling young flesh, butchering it when old.

40 He will be infamous for slaughtering,
will leave so few that centuries will pass
before the state of Florence is restored."

43 This coming woe showed on the troubled face
of he announcing it and he who heard.
Said I, "If you want word of that conveyed

46 to Earth below, I'd better know your names."
Chief spokesman of the two replied, "You ask
what you denied to me. I can't refuse,

for you are in God's grace. Know that in life
I, Guido del Duca, felt so much spite
at sight of folk enjoying life, my face

swelled and turned scarlet in my jealous rage.
I sowed bad seed, now chew the bitter crop.
No wonder I am blind, for envy's whip

drove me away from human fellowship,
engrossing good things for myself and heirs.
O humankind, our mad wish NOT to share

repels the sympathy and love we need,
brings endless war. You Tuscans know that well.
Rinier of the house of Calboli

is my companion, last true nobleman
of an old family. None after he
have been or will be good, and this is true

of every great family between
mountains and Po from Reno to the sea.
Once they were generous and chivalrous.

Art, sport, good manners flourished under them.
Now fields of their estates grow fouler weeds
than decades of good farming can repair.

Where now exist Arrigo Mainardi,
Guido di Carpigna, good Lizio,
also the good Pierre Traversaro?

In the Romagna a vile bastard race
replaces every one; and when again
will a Fabbro be found in Bologna?

A Fosco in Faenza? – noble sprout
from a most humble herb. Do not wonder,
Tuscan, if now I weep recalling how

Guido da Prata, Ugulino d'Azzo
lived and ruled, Tignoso and company,
the Traversaro and Anastagi,

both now without an heir. O Tuscan, think!
I knew these knights, these ladies moved by love
and courtesy, where now is villainy.

O Bertinoro, why do you remain?
Your lords abandoned your corrupt old den –
follow them! Bagnacavallo does well

in failing to breed men. Castrocaro
does ill, Conio worse by breeding lords
deserving Heaven's curse. The Pagani

still keep old honesty, or will when free
of that sly fiend Malnardo, even so
their name cannot regain its ancient fame.

O Hugo Fantolini, your good name
is safe since no one now possesses it.
Tuscan, depart. I'd rather weep than speak,

our conversation has so wrung my heart."
We knew that these dear spirits heard us go.
Their silence made us sure our way was right.

A mighty cry suddenly cleft the air:
"All seeing who I am desire my death!"
Before our ears recovered from that shout

another deafening outcry burst out,
too loud to be an echo of the first:
"I am Aglauros who was turned to stone."

Silence returned. Instead of following
I stepped beside my guide. Without surprise
he saw the question in my eyes and said

"You have heard Cain, his brother's murderer,
and sister-killing Aglauros. These two
are reins to hold back human jealousy,

if we will bite God's bit on Earth below,
but most prefer His enemy's sweet bait,
whose hook then pulls them downward into Hell,

while those who wish to see can raise their eyes
to starry wheels of Heaven high above,
created beautiful, given in love,

inviting all to soar into the skies."

15: Ascent to the Wrathful

1 Each starry and each planetary sphere
circles the Earth, running like child at play
over and under us from day to day.

4 Although it was midnight in Italy
the time was now late afternoon when we,
rounding the hill, walked west toward the sun

7 and level with it, so it warmed my face
pleasantly, till new dazzlement ahead
caused me to raise my hands and shield my sight,

10 and cry aloud, "What radiance is this?"
"All Heaven's housekeepers bring extra light,"
said he. "This one beckons to the next stair.

13 The sight of such will soon not dazzle you
but give as much delight as you can bear."
We neared that angel and I saw he stood

16 where in the cliff a flight of steps began
broader, less steep than any we had known.
A glad angelic voice said, "Enter there,"

19 while his angelic finger pointed up.
We bowed our heads, set feet upon the stair
and climbing heard him very sweetly sing

the fifth beatitude of Jesus Christ:
Blessed are the merciful, followed by
You who have overcome a sin, rejoice.

Since we were now ascending side by side
I thought to profit by my master's speech.
"You are the voice of reason and my guide,"

I said to him, "so please will you explain
what Guido of Romagna meant when he,
blinded for envy, spoke of partnership?"

Said Virgil, "He now knows the social cost
of his worst sin, and so condemns it most.
When goods are kept instead of being shared

goods become selfish gain, so fear of loss
drives owners to care nothing for the pain
and poverty they cause by seizing more –

more than they need out of the public store
of goodness God has given everyone
our common Earth. The more that folk say *ours*

instead of *mine*, the more their charity."
I said, "Forgive me, but I cannot see
why riches some enjoy deprive the rest."

Said he, "Your worldly greed has blinded you,
for property makes darkness of God's light.
True charity enlarges all we share.

Like sunshine, love enriches all it shows.
If these words do not satisfy your need
to know how Heaven's justice works, then wait

49 ’til you meet Beatrice, who will wholly
supply that craving more than I can do.
Two wounds upon your brow are now erased.

52 Strive to erase five more, though healing them
will cause some pain.” I was about to say
“Your words have satisfied”, when suddenly

55 we reached the topmost stair where I was
silenced by my eyes. They were surprised
by a vision of a congregation,

58 in a great temple. A woman there wore
a sweet maternal look and meekly asked,
“Son, why treat us so? Father and I feared

61 you were lost before we found you here.”
She said no more, vanished, was replaced by
a woman with a fretful tear-wet face

64 crying aloud resentfully, “Husband!
Pisistratus! Athens’ almighty lord!
Are you content that a youth publicly

67 kisses our daughter without punishment?”
I thought I saw smiling Pisistratus
and heard his calm reply: “If I punish

70 those who love me and mine, how will I treat
others who offer hate?” Then I beheld
a frantic mob all yelling, “Kill! Kill! Kill!”

73 while stoning a youth sinking to the ground
praying in his death agonies that God
pardon his enemies. Realities

claimed my mind again. I found my master 76
held my arm as he remarked, “As if drunk,
with shut eyes you have walked for half a league.”

Said I, “But I saw visions! Let me explain . . .” 79
“No need, for if you wore a hundred masks
I would still know your thoughts,” said he.

“Those visions should have taught you to accept 82
waters of peace from God’s eternal source.
I spoke of how you walked upon this road

only to wake you up, put conscious force 85
into what had been blindly stumbling feet.
A dreaming pilgrim sometimes needs a prod.”

We walked on through the evening, gazing ahead, 88
when there sped to us from the setting sun
an airborne shred of what seemed smoke or fog

followed by larger darker shreds, and then 91
dense black cloud overtook them and us too.
There was no escape. Spreading everywhere

it robbed us both of sight and the pure air. 94

16: The Wrathful

1 The gloom of night and Hell hid Heaven's light
more wholly than the thickest curtain could
and stung my eyes. Again I shut them tight.

4 My trusty guide offered his shoulder now,
told me to take good hold and not let go,
so in a blind man's state I went ahead

7 led through foul air while he kept telling me
to have great care we did not separate.
Then voices came, singing sweet harmony

10 in prayers for peace and mercy, and each one
beginning with these words, *O Lamb of God.*
"Master," I asked "are these souls penitent?"

13 "Quite right," said he. "By vocal unity
they untie knots of wrath still binding them,
preventing progress on their upward path."

16 A new voice spoke: "Who are you walking through
our smoke, talking as though months and years still
measured time for you?" My master told me,

19 "Answer, and ask how to get out of here."
I said, "O soul cleansing yourself of sin
till fit to face Him who created you,

if you keep company with us I'll tell
what brings us here. It is astonishing."
He said, "I will – as far as Heaven allows.

Hearing will join us, though we cannot see.
So now, astonish me." "I am not dead,"
said I, "though I have travelled here through Hell.

God's grace demands I see His Heavenly court,
a strange idea to modern ears, but true.
Who were you when alive? And if you know

where the next stair is, please escort us there."
"I was a Lombard. Marco was my name.
I knew the world yet loved the good at which

people no longer aim or greatly love.
To climb up higher go straight on," said he,
adding, "Please pray for me when you're elsewhere."

"I promise that," I said, "but dreadful doubt
of human virtue, doubled by your words,
is swelling me. If I don't speak it out

I will explode. Your view of things confirms
what Guido of Romagna said below –
the world is overwhelmed by wickedness.

Folk break God's laws. Help me to see the cause
that I can make it known. Astrologers
blame stars for our sins." He cried out "Brother,

alas! Be not as blind as those!" Sighing
he said, "We would have no *choice* if ruled by
blind necessity. Each would be a part

of process without consciousness! Justice!
Joy in doing well! Misery for sin!
Our sense of choice is fact, like sense of light,

sound, heat, weight, pleasure, pain. Denying one
rejects all common sense reality.
Appetites are from Heaven and therefore good,

but lead to greed if wrongly understood.
Our senses let us work out what is right
and so oppose mistaken appetite.

Strengthened by exercise this virtuous fight
conquers all things, making a free new mind
just limited by what is nearer God.

If the world goes astray, then search within!
Find in yourself the root and source of sin.
As you want guidance let me be your guide.

Listen. When a tiny soul comes from the hand
of Him who loved it while creating it,
the soul knows nothing. The joyful maker

lets it move eagerly to take delight
in many small things, some of which are bad.
Thus it needs parents who will curb it well,

direct it to the best things it should love.
Thus we need laws and kings enforcing them,
priesthoods who point to New Jerusalem,

the happy state God wills us to create.
That is why he makes laws. Who do they curb?
None. None. Our shepherds do not lead their flocks

by peaceful waters and through pastures green
where they may safely graze. They fleece their sheep
and sell the wool for gain. When people see

their leaders worship wealth they too adore,
greed multiplies itself. All fight for more.
Bad government makes Earth a wicked place –

nature is not corrupt. There was a time
when Rome strove hard to make the whole world good.
Two grand authorities like double suns

showed men the laws of Earth and laws of God.
These quell each other now. When King and Pope
equally try to wield the sword and crook,

neither corrects or fears the other one.
Observe the modern state of Italy!
Courage and courtesy were here before

King Frederick attacked the papacy,
which fought back just like he. Now you may go
by Arno, Tiber, Adige and Po

nor fear to meet with honest company.
Just three old men do well in ancient ways
and won't be there for long: good Gherardo,

Conrad di Palazzo, also Guido
da Castel, all famed for their honesty.
Tell people that the Church of Rome's attempt

to seize both Heavenly and Earthly power
corrupts itself, corrupting others too."
"I see you're right," I said, "and also see

103 why Hebrew law forbad that Levi's sons
(the Jewish priests) inherit property.
But who is this Gherardo that you say

106 still shows old virtues to this rotten age?"
"You puzzle me," said he. "Your speech is Tuscan.
Surely all Tuscans know good Gherardo?

109 I won't say more of him except to give
his daughter Gaia's name. God bless you both.
Here now, alas, we have to part since I

112 see light through smoke ahead, and so goodbye."

17: On and Up

Those who have been in mountain mists too thick
for eyes to pierce, then seen them thinning down
to let the sun show as a small, pale disc,

know how the setting sun appeared to me
as the thick fog dispersed. Shorn of bright rays
it hung above the sea, while far below

dim shadows hid the shores. As we walked on
imaginary visions mastered me,
visions of ancient anger and past wrong,

so great that I believe no trumpet blast,
or stormy thunderclap, however strong
could have recalled my eyes to where I was.

Procne appeared, changed to a swallow's form
for punishing unfaithful Tereus
by feeding him their son, baked in a pie.

Then I beheld another fantasy
of Haman, fierce and scornful, hanging high,
thus rightly punished by an angry king

for outrage against Jewish Mordecai.
Lastly I saw a daughter's wild despair
at sight of mother who had hanged herself

because the man her daughter was to wed,
Prince Turnus, had been slaughtered in a fight.
As sleep is broken when a sudden light

strikes through a dream, a brightness wakened me
whiter, more dazzling than the sun at noon.
On looking round to see just where I stood

a gentle voice said, “Here is your ascent.”
This drove away all other thought, but though
longing to look upon the speaker’s face

its brightness baffled me. My leader said,
“This angel showing us the upward way
without us asking, hides in his own light.

Accept his courtesy. Climb upstairs now.
We cannot move at all when it is night.”
My foot was on the uphill path’s first step

when a wing brushed my face, a soft voice said,
“Blest are peacemakers, free of sinful wrath.”
As we went up, the setting sun’s last rays

were slanting steep. On each side stars appeared.
“O strength!” I inward groaned, “Why disappear?”,
for as we reached the highest step my weight

felt heavier than stone. We both sank down
like boats left high and dry upon a beach.
I listened and heard nothing, asked at last,

“Dear Master, say what sin is purging here?
Our legs can’t move. Don’t let that stop your tongue.”
He answered thus: “Sloth prevents energy

achieving what it should, so here you'll see
how healthy active love must be restored.
Listen and pluck good fruit from our delay.

Since love is God's creative force, all things
(time, space, star, sun, earth, insect, human child)
keep going by God's love. Love has two kinds:

the natural, and of the mind. Mistakes
are never natural. Only minds can err,
loving wrong things, or good ones with too much

or with too little force. Thus love brings both
good deeds and deeds requiring punishment.
When we attend to God, the Source of All,

our desires are kept in proper measure.
We are not then seduced by sinful pleasure,
until we look away and therefore stray.

As none can harm the source of what they are
(trying to wound the sun would be as mad)
the only law of God that we can break

is that which says, *Love neighbour as yourself,*
the rule for Jews that Moses carved in stone
and God when born as Man gave to us all.

And so the only evil folk can love
is harming other folk in three main ways
you know by having seen them punished below:

first, trying to excel by doing down
those by our side – perversions born of pride.
Second, by fear of losing wealth or fame

76 when those nearby do well – envy's the name.
Lastly, when insult, real or by mistake
inflames blind anger hungry for revenge.

79 You know these states of lamentable love.
Think now of those you'll see lamenting here
who loved true good with insufficient zeal,

82 and higher still you'll find three kinds of grief
endured for not loving the best stuff well.
I leave you to work these out for yourself.

85 My son, believe me, I have said enough."

18: Love and Sloth

Silent once more, my teacher closely watched 1
my face for understanding of his words.
Though thirsting to hear more I held my tongue

lest further questioning would pester him. 4
That good instructor guessed what I suppressed.
With smile and nod he told me to ask more.

“Master,” said I, “you clarify my brain, 7
so say again how love induces both
virtuous actions and their opposite.”

“Give me your full attention now,” said he, 10
“and concentrate your analytic mind
on truth that Plato gave humanity

before Epictetus made scholars blind. 13
All souls are born with appetite for love,
so bound to look at what most seems to please

whenever pleasure beckons them, and thus 16
attractive visions from outside ourselves
enter our souls. Love is what draws them in,

makes soul and vision a new entity. 19
Thus nature’s objects take a hold of soul,
and as the flames leap upward to the sun

22 (the source of every fire) no soul can rest
before she blends with objects that she loves.
But they are wrong who say all love is good.

25 Substantial minds possess material shapes
and yet are different, though only seen
in what they do and show, like grass when green.

28 None know how virtue starts. It moves our hearts
as bees are moved to building honeycomb.
No praise for such instinctive skill is due,

31 because such instincts should not be obeyed
till brought in tune with other wills as right
and communal, as are the busy bees.

34 We have to choose between bad love and good
by freely reasoning, as all folk can
when love submits to reason as it should.

37 Indeed, necessity creates our love,
but free-will only gives it right control.
Reason and free-willed souls are gifts from God

40 to everyone: Greek, Roman, Pagan, Jew
and those like you born since that hero died
who conquered death. My words sound cut and dried.

43 They point to Heaven's Grace but they stop short
at gate of Paradise, where that pure soul
Beatrice will become your only guide."

46 Now it was midnight and the rising moon
upon the wane had reached its height, and hung
among the stars like tilted golden bowl.

The poet who had brought his birthplace fame
now dropped the burden of instructing me.
As we reclined I pondered drowsily

on all the noble thought he had made mine,
till noises at my back awakened me,
for round the mountain track there came a mob

who seemed at first a wildly charging herd
of peasants drunk on half-fermented wine,
but as they neared I saw most were well dressed.

Not revelry but pain was driving them,
a frantic pain allowing them no rest.
I and my guide, our energy renewed,

sprang to our feet and sprinted at the side
of two in front who alternately cried,
"Hail Mary, pregnant with our Saviour,

rushing uphill to greet her cousin Beth!"
and, "Caesar, in haste to conquer Lerida,
routed Marseilles and then swooped into Spain."

Meanwhile the horde behind were shouting out,
"Go faster! Faster still! Slowness in love
prevents the Grace that blesses from above!"

My master cried, "Your mighty urgency,
O souls, will one day purge the laziness
delaying your salvation when alive,

but this man lives. Heaven has ordered him
to climb above you when the sun appears.
Please teach us how to reach the nearest stair."

Someone among these racers answered him,
"Follow us. You will see a staircase soon.
Forgive me if I have to run away

and seem discourteous. I lived in great
Emperor Barbarossa's day, he who
plundered Milan. I was then abbot of

San Zeno in Verona, and can say
who rules it now has one foot in the grave,
and soon in Hell will curse what he has done.

He has made certain that his bastard son,
crippled in legs and mind, will take his place,
keeping a good priest from that benefice . . ."

He raced so far ahead I heard no more,
but I was glad to recollect his words
before my master said, "Now look behind.

Here come the two who goad the slothful on
by telling them some things to keep in mind."
At once I heard a strong voice loudly say,

"Of those to whom the Red Sea opened wide,
three only lived to see The Promised Land
because of slothfulness upon the way."

Another cried, "When Aeneas led forth
his Trojan band to the grand enterprise
of founding Rome, many abandoned him

in Sicily, and died there without fame."
I paused then till that multitude had passed
quite out of sight. My head was in a whirl.

Each thought that came inspired another one 103
or two, or three that contradicted it
with hectic fancies, frivolous or deep,

until I sank beside the road, asleep. 106

19: To the Avaricious

In a cold hour before the vast dark cone
of shadow we call night is split by dawn,
I dreamed I was approached by a foul crone,

hunch-backed, club-footed, hands like vulture claws,
bald-headed, stammering from drooling lips.
Her wrinkled skin was corpse-like yellow-grey.

I stared and saw her change like frosty field
with bright sun warming it. Her skin grew smooth,
blushing a lovely rose. She stood up slim,

erect. Her young face kindly smiled on me,
framed by rich locks of chestnut-coloured hair.
Her soft throat crooned so blithe an air, my ears

drank each note eagerly. Here's what she sang.
"I am Sirena. Sailors love my voice,
leaving the sea for joy on land with me.

My singing stopped Ulysses wandering,
and none I satisfy try to depart."
Before that sweet sound died a stern voice cried

"O Virgil Virgil Virgil, what is *that*?"
I found a stately lady at my side
glaring on Sirena indignantly.

Virgil appeared, saw my companion
and then abruptly stripped Sirena bare.
The belly he exposed gave off such stink

it wakened me. I sat up. There he stood
saying, "I've called you thrice. Let's find the stair."
I rose and saw the day was well begun,

light flooding all the circles of the hill.
We marched right on the road where the bright sun
now cast my shade ahead. I stared at it

with downcast, brooding face, my body bent
like half a bridge's arch until I heard,
"Here now you may ascend", in tones more sweet

than spoken by the tongue of any friend.
An angel pointed to an opening
between two walls of flinty stone. He said,

"Blessèd are mourners: they shall be consoled,"
and as we passed, fanned us with swanlike wings.
When we had passed above the angel's head,

my master asked, "What's wrong with you?" I said,
"A recent dream has filled me full of fear."
He answered, "That old hag you saw was she

who makes all those above us weep. You saw
how to reject her – be content with that.
Strike heels into the earth and climb! Look up!

Beyond that blue, God's starry wheels revolve."
The hooded falcon stares down at its feet,
but when released, soars up into the sky.

49 Now like that bird was I. Sped by desire
I ran right up that stair to the fifth ledge,
then stopped astonished. Where the road swept round

52 folk laid out flat covered each foot of ground,
face down in dirt. They sobbed words hard to hear
but I made out, "We sold our souls for dust."

55 My master cried, "O you whom God permits
repentance by such pains, I truly know
Justice and Hope have saved you from despair.

58 We pass among you to a greater height.
Will someone please tell us a shortcut there?"
From just ahead of us a voice replied,

61 "Since you are free from having to lie prone,
walk with right hand toward the outer rim."
My master saw my eyes imploring him,

64 knew what I asked and nodded his consent.
Stooping beside that unpurged sufferer
I said, "Please tell me of the man you were.

67 I know the more repentant tears you shed,
will bring you sooner into Paradise,
but for a little time tell me instead

70 why you must lie with backside to the sky.
Say too if I may serve you in some way,
when I at last return to Italy."

73 "I'll tell you why Heaven turns me upside down,"
said he, "but speak first of the man I was
before elected to the papacy.

Into the Gulf of Genoa there flows
a limpid river down a pleasant glen
called Lavagna, which also is a name

my people used and I inherited
from count and cardinal no better than
the other priests whose greed disgrace the Church.

But when Saint Peter's shoes were on my feet
a purer spirit suddenly was mine,
too late! Too late I struggled with the weight

of the Pope's mantle. For one short month
and a few days I tried to shake it free
of parasites who clung as I had done.

That struggle killed me. It will save my soul
when I have cleaned the foul thing I've become:
a creature given up to selfish greed.

Here is my punishment. There is no worse
pain on this Holy Mountain. We refused
to see the shining multitude of stars.

Enchanted by our wilful avarice
we fixed our eyes downward on Earthly things,
so Justice now must clamp us here face down

quite motionless in dirt, as in a vice.
This distress was our own choice! Tears alone
can wash away the dirt I partly am,

freeing what God created me to be."
I knelt and he, sensing my reverence
demanded, "Why do you lower yourself?"

103 "I have to bow. I cannot stand," said I,
"before your dignity in suffering."
He commanded, "Brother, straighten your legs!

106 I am like you and all of us, servant
of only One. There is no slavery
or mastery for equals under God,

109 who calls His Pope *servant of my servants*,
which several forget. And now please go.
You asked if you could serve me down on Earth.

112 My niece Alagia is thriving there.
Let her know what and why I suffer here.
Her inborn goodness can relieve my soul.

115 Uncle in Purgatory tells her so."

20: Hoarders and Wasters

While thirsting for more words with that good Pope
I found his silence stronger than my will,
so had to leave before I'd drunk my fill.

Between the prostrate mourners and cliff base
a narrow space left something like a path.
I paced along this, close behind my guide,

appalled by lamentations on our right
from those who now felt greed's iniquity.
To Hell, you wolf of Greed! Your poisoned fangs

have damned more souls than any other beasts!
Your gluttony enforces poverty.
You spread starvation by your wasteful feasts.

Having to place our footsteps carefully
we slowly moved along this narrow way,
then from in front we heard a clear voice cry,

"Sweet Mary!" Like a woman giving birth
in agony that yet suggested joy,
adding, "What could exceed the poverty

of labour pains within a trough of hay,
between the muzzles of an ox and ass?"
A pause, then the voice said, "Fabricius

chose virtue and poverty, not riches
by military conquest. So should we."
Wanting to see the soul who said these things

I pressed ahead, hearing him talk about
Saint Nicholas, whose generosity
brought marriage to the poorest of young maids.

I said, "O soul in pain announcing good,
please tell me who you were. Your words will be
recorded down on Earth when I return."

Said he, "I will reply, though not because
your good report will do the Earth much good.
You have a radiance that pleases me.

From me sprang up that monarchy of France
which overshadows Christendom and stops
much good fruit growing there. If Douai, Lille,

Ghent, Bruges had strength, they'd cast it off,
for which I pray to He who judges All.
In Paris Dad was butcher. I became

head of the royal household when the last
of Charlemagne's great line, a monk, expired.
I had such wealth and friends that very soon

my son was wedded to the widowed queen.
From me, Hugh Capet, grew that lengthy line
of Philips, Louises, commanding France,

their bones entombed in consecrated earth.
As long as they inherited Provence,
they did no good and very little harm

but riches strengthened their rapacity. 49
To further it, by force and fraud they took
Ponthieu and Normandy and Gascony,

then went beyond, killing in Italy 52
Conradin, and better still, poisoning
Saint Thomas Aquinas. Soon you will see

another prince to bring my France more fame. 55
Using hypocrisy (that Judas lance)
he will burst in the guts of Florence,

gaining no land by it but gold and shame. 58
The less he thinks of this, the worse for him.
His brother sells his daughter to an old

and evil count, also for gold. O Greed, 61
what fouler misdeeds can you bring my race?
To make these crimes seem less, I can foresee

the fleur-de-lis flag enter Anagni, 64
see Christ's appointed Vicar, captured, mocked,
fed with vinegar and slain between

two live thieves by a new Pontius Pilate 67
so unscrupulous, he goes on to loot
the treasury that good Knights Templar use,

escorting pilgrims to Jerusalem. 70
O Lord my God, when shall I gladly see
your vengeance smiting down these evil men?

You heard me calling on the Holy Ghost's 73
one Virgin Bride. By day we think of Her
and others without greed; at night we brood

76 on those whose sin resembled ours, such as
Pygmalion, traitor, thief, parricide
through lust for gold; Midas, whose silly greed

79 made him ridiculous – a king with ass's ears.
We think of foolish Achan stoned to death
for keeping gold Joshua meant for God;

82 Ananias and Saphira his wife,
stealing coin from the first Christian kirks,
and dropping dead, rebuked. We praise the kicks

85 the angel's horse gave Heliodorus
when by force he tried to steal the treasure
from Jerusalem's temple. We lastly

88 shout in chorus, "Crassus, how does gold taste?"
remembering Rome's grasping millionaire
whose mouth and throat a Parthian monarch filled

91 with molten gold. Sometimes we yell aloud
or softly sing the stories that we share,
or ponder them. You heard me praising Mary.

94 Others were also thinking of her then."
We parted from him, trying to walk fast,
but suddenly the whole great mountain shook

97 as if it fell. I felt a deathly chill.
Delos, floating island, quaked not more
when sunk and fixed by Jupiter, to be

100 a birthplace for the gods of sun and moon.
Mourners on every side shouted aloud.
My master drew me close, said, "Do not fear,

for I am guiding you." Then I made out
from the folk nearest us the words they cried
were *Gloria in Excelsis Deo.*

Like shepherds who first heard this news proclaimed
we stood stock-still and stupefied until
they shut their mouths. The mountain ceased to shake.

Again we walked upon the narrow path
beside those spirits weeping as before.
Never did ignorance make me so keen

to understand, or so afraid to ask.

21: Statius

1 The thirst for truth not to be satisfied
until Christ quench it was tormenting me.
I picked my steps upon that awkward way

4 while grieving for the mourners' long delay
when all at once I noticed we were three.
Luke writes of how two followers of Christ

7 after his crucifixion, found themselves
joined on a road by One they did not know
at first, or recognise as He. We two

10 were overtaken from behind, nor knew
until we heard, "Brothers, God send you peace."
Said Virgil, "May you find it with the bless'd

13 in that high court of God which exiles me."
"But why?" the stranger asked as we walked on,
"If you are still excluded from God's Grace,

16 how did you climb so high on Heaven's stair?"
At this my poet said, "See this man's face!
It still has marks the angel at the gate

19 wrote on his brow. He'll reach a greater place
though still his thread of life is being spun.
Death has not slit it yet. His soul – sister

of yours and mine – could not climb here alone, 22
having no eyes like ours. I was released
from Limbo as his guide and do my best.

But can you tell what shook this sacred hill? 25
What made it ring with shouts of jubilee?"
These questions chimed so well with my desires

I listened for the answers eagerly. 28
The shade replied, "Nothing disorderly
like rain, dew, hail, frost, snow can rise above

the three steps where Saint Peter's curate sits. 31
To wind and lightning also we're immune
and subterranean shocks. What moves us

is a soul released by love from sin, 34
free at last to rise where it wants to be.
I lay in pain over five hundred years,

and my release is a most glad surprise. 37
You felt the tremor, heard the shout of praise
from the devout. God send them soon above!"

The drink is more enjoyed the worse the thirst. 40
How this intelligence delighted me!
My wise guide said, "I now perceive the cords

of conscience that hold these mourners down, 43
have been untied for you, hence jubilee.
Please tell us who you were, and why you were

thus pinioned down for many centuries." 46
"I lived when Titus was our Emperor,
he who made deadly warfare on the Jews.

49 My gift of song was such that from Toulouse,
Rome drew me to itself, and placed the crown
of myrtle on my brow for poetry.

52 My name's still spoken there – it's Statius.
I sang the wars of Thebes: and tried to make
Achilles hero of an epic song,

55 but that was rather more than I could do.
The spark that kindled my poetic aim
leapt from the flame of Virgil's *Aeneid*,

58 where many other poets have caught fire.
He taught me how heroic history,
the strife of gods and men in daily life

61 is the pure substance of morality.
Without his *Aeneid* none would believe
my verses worth a penny. Could I live

64 when Virgil lived I gladly would endure,
what? . . . an extra Purgatorial year."
These words turned Virgil to me with a look

67 that silently said, "Silence!" Willpower
cannot do all. Laughter and tears are so
near passions causing them, sometimes they show

70 whether we will or no. I only smiled,
at which the spirit looked into my eyes,
where most expression is, and said, "Forgive,

73 but I must ask what caused that gleam of mirth?"
Between command for silence and these words
begging for speech, what could I do? I sighed.

My master understood for he too sighed
and said, “Reply. Answer his eagerness.”
“You wondered, ancient spirit, at my smiling,”

I began. “Hear now a greater wonder.
He leading me is he who taught you how
to sing of gods and men – Virgil, I mean.

I only smiled because you spoke of him.”
Statius, stooped to cuddle Virgil’s feet,
was told by him, “Brother, that can’t be done.

We both of us are shades, so bodiless,
and neither nobler than the other one.”
Statius, rising, said, “It proves my love

that I forgot we lack solidity.”

22: To the Gluttonous

1 We three then passed the angel of the stair
taking us up to the next mountain ledge,
but not before his wing brushed from my brow

4 the scar of the fifth P, as he announced,
"*Blessèd are they that thirst for righteousness.*"
Lighter of foot than I had ever felt,

7 I followed easily these two swift souls
conversing as they climbed; heard Virgil say,
"All good and selfless love inspires a love

10 reflecting it. I heard from Juvenal
(who came to Limbo and had been your friend)
how highly you regarded me, also

13 he praised your work so much I thought of you
far more than others I have never met.
I hope you will consider me a friend

16 if I ask something many might think rude.
How came (with all the wisdom you possessed)
the sin of avarice to foul your breast?

19 You need not answer. That is understood."
Statius smiled a little at these words
then answered, "All you say declares your love,

although appearances have led astray. 22
Because I lay face downward in the grit
among the hoarders, I appeared like one.

My sin, however, was the opposite. 25
I was a wastrel, spending money fast
to glut my appetites: a jolly sin

I thought, but squandering is just as bad 28
as hoarding money tightly in a bank.
That I'm not where wasters jostle hoarders

endlessly in Hell, I have you to thank, 31
for in your *Aeneid*'s third book I read
To what crimes have not many been misled

by that infernal appetite for gold? 34
This made me stop and think because I saw
that if I did not rectify my flaw

I'd sink to be more beastly than I was." 37
"I'm puzzled by another mystery,"
my master said. "Your Theban epic deals

with history, but gives no hint of Faith, 40
lacking which no good effort sets us free.
Faith releases you from prison here

to find (as I will not) a higher home. 43
Some guide in Rome directed you into
Saint Peter's holy ark, which has no place

within your poems. Why?" Statius said, 46
"Cowardice stopped me emulating you,
in your third Eclogue heralding the birth

of one whose reign would bring us peace on Earth
and happily restore true Golden Age,
creating thus a better human race.

You died before our Saviour was born,
I lived after the Resurrection.
Your poetry first made of me a poet,

then taught me how to be a Christian
in days when there were preachers of Christ's faith,
and these I visited. Their upright ways

soon taught me to despise all other sects
so I was baptised when Domitian
was persecuting theirs. I meanly chose

to seem a Pagan still. Four centuries
I raced around the slothful circle till
my lukewarmness for that was purged away.

Now say (if there is still time as we go)
where that old Latin author Terence is,
and Plautus, Cecilius, Varius.

Are these damned? And in what place?" My guide said,
"In Limbo, where I meet them face to face
with that great blind Greek Homer, he

whose genius gave new life to all the arts,
with thinkers, playwrights and historians,
and the heroic folk of whom they wrote."

The poets, having reached the topmost stair,
were not quite sure which way to turn until
my teacher said, "Let us go to the right."

They did. I followed very close behind,
learning much from their talk of poetry
how I should write my own. And then we saw

a tall tree in the middle of the road
with many fruits whose scent was sweet and good.
As a fir tapers from great width to height

this tapered downward, so could not be climbed.
From the high cliff upon the left a stream
of pure clear water fell among the boughs

which, glistening, absorbed it while a voice
among them cried, “You may not eat this food!”
It added, “Mary, at the marriage feast,

cared more for nourishment of other guests
than for her mouth, and anciently in Rome
women preferred pure water for their drink.

By hungering the prophet Daniel
grew wiser still. In the first Golden Age
hunger made acorns seem the sweetest food.

The Baptist thought honey and locusts good.”

23: The Gluttons

1 I gazed aloft through the green foliage
like hawker who wastes hours pursuing birds
until my more-than-father said, "Come, son!

4 Make better use of time." Turning my face
and running after him I heard a hymn
sung by a chorus mingling joy and pain:

7 "Lord, open up our lips." I asked my guide,
"Father, please tell me what this signifies."
Said he, "Souls paying God what is His due."

10 Like travellers absorbed in thought who rush
by others with one quick enquiring look,
so, coming from behind and speeding on,

13 a crowd, silent and devout, overtook
and passed us with astonished stares. Their eyes
were deeply sunk, their white skins clung tight

16 to bones beneath. Erysichthon who gnawed
his limbs when wild with hunger was as gaunt,
and those starved in Jerusalem's great siege

19 where Miriam ate her child. Skull sockets
seemed gemless rings. The nose-bone M was plain
to any who read OMO in a face.

I knew not why the sight and scent of fruit
had famished them, but greatly wondered at
their harsh emaciation, scabbiness,

and agony. One turned his eyes on me
and cried, "Rejoice! What goodness brings you here?"
Not by his looks I knew him, but his voice –

he was my friend, Forese Donati.
"Ignore," he begged, "my withered skin and flesh.
Please tell me about you. Who are the two

you travel with? You must explain all this."
"I wept to see your face when dead," I said,
"and weep to see it now. In God's name say

what starves you? Upset by your present state,
I don't see how to answer questions yet."
"The spring of water nourishing that tree,"

said he, "makes me as lean as all of us
who sing as we pass under branches of
that fragrant fruit and spray. It renews our

hunger and thirst. We glutted appetite
to such excess in life these painful pangs
are needed to restore our holiness.

It feels like pain but is a comfort too,
bringing us closer to the tree where One
who died to make us free was crucified –

our Lord Himself." I said, "But Forese,
you only died five years ago. I know
you were not very bad, but men as good

49 are waiting centuries outside the gate
before admitted to ascend the stairs.
What lets you come so fast and far?" He said,

52 "My widow Nelly's tears and constant prayers,
heard in the court where love is highest law.
She's that rare thing among our womenfolk,

55 a widow who still loves the man she wed
and does not seek romps in another bed.
Her prayers have raised me up and through the gate

58 and stairs above to here. She's one of few.
The savage women of Sardinia
are chaste beside most female Florentines.

61 Brother, I prophesy an evil time
when priests from holy pulpits will denounce
our noble dames for how they flaunt their tits.

64 I hear that Muslim wives dress modestly,
and wives from equally barbaric shores
need none to tell them not to dress like whores.

67 I wish they saw ahead what tragedies
will come before their baby boys grow beards.
Dear brother, it is time to tell your tale

70 not just to me: also my company.
Your shadow on the road amazes them."
At that I said, "Farese, I will not

73 give tongue to all we did when we were young.
I left such wildness just four days ago
when my best teacher led me bodily

through Hell then up to here, circling this hill 76
that straightens folk made crooked by bad will.
He'll be my guide till I meet Beatrice.

He is Virgil, the other Statius 79
for whom all Purgatory shook like mad
releasing him, as you will one day be.

How great that both of us can now be glad." 82

24: Toward Temperance

1 This conversation did not slow us down.
We went on like a yacht before fair winds.
The former gluttons who appeared twice dead

4 found us astonishing. Continuing,
I said, "Please speak of how Piccarda is,
and of these gazing, may I know their names?"

7 "My lovely sister is in Paradise,"
said he, "as for the rest of us, although
almost featureless from fasting, none seek

10 anonymity. There is" (he pointed)
"Bonagiunta, poet and toper
of Lucca. He with the most wizened face

13 is Martin, Pope, Defender of our Faith,
who died because he over-ate the eels
of Bolsena, stewed in sweet Vernage wine . . ."

16 He mentioned more who did not seem ashamed
but pleased by my attention: Ubaldin
de la Pila who made new recipes

19 and now from hunger bites the air; Archbishop
Boniface who kept a mighty table;
Lord Marquess of Fornay whose thirst got worse

the more he drank; but Bonagiuta
of Lucca seemed most keen to speak with me.
I turned to him again. From his dry throat

the word “Gentucca” came. “I do not know,”
said I, “what that means. Can you speak more plain?”
“A woman born but not yet wed,” said he,

“will make the town of Lucca kind to you.
If you don’t understand that, never mind.
Thus it shall be. Let us now speak of verse.

Surely you wrote the poem which begins,
Ladies who have intelligence of love.
That was a splendid novelty. Your lines

have sweetness, strength, passionate nakedness
that almost made me blush.” I shrugged, replied,
“I write as love commands.” He cried aloud,

“Yes, that is why you beat a poor old bard:
like me, and he they call the Notary
of Sicily, and Tuscan Guittone.

Compared with yours our style is cold and hard.
Our grandest efforts were just good enough
to point you on the way to better stuff,

but love is what has made your lines excel.”
Then he fell silent with a sigh and smile.
Cranes wintering upon the Nile take wing

to fly much faster in a single line.
So too the former gluttons rearranged
to travel forward at a swifter pace.

49 As some let others race ahead while they
regain their breath, Forese paused to ask,
"How long before we meet again?" I said,

52 "I do not know how long I have to live
but think my healthy years ahead are few.
Our Florence mocks at virtue, praises sin,

55 and hurries down the road to ruin's brink."
Said he, "And one who'll help to push her in
is my own brother, Corso Donati,

58 and he will meet his end by being tossed
and dragged behind his horse along the ground.
Dear friend, farewell. I must exert myself

61 to make up for the precious time I've lost."
With lengthened stride he disappeared ahead.
Beside these captains of the human mind

64 I followed at a slower pace behind
until the curving road brought into sight
another tree fruit-laden like the first.

67 A mob with arms stretched upward underneath
were begging, though I could not hear their speech.
The tree, like adult teasing greedy child,

70 wagged fruit above their grabbing fingers' reach
until the starving grabbers ran away.
As Virgil, Statius and I drew near

73 a voice out of the leaves commanded us,
"Go forward! On the summit of this hill
you'll see the tree whose fruit made Eve so ill.

This is a shoot from it. Recall fights lost
by those who gave way to their appetites:
drunken centaurs Theseus had to slay;

the Jews whom Gideon chose not to use
because they quenched their thirst incautiously."
At foot of inner cliff we picked our way,

hearing more punishments for gluttony.
We walked on far beyond that second tree
in sombre meditation without talk

until another voice astonished me:
"What are you three thinking of?" Timidly
I raised my head, beheld a figure glow

more red than furnace-heated glass or steel.
"If you would go above, turn here," it said.
"This stairway is for people seeking peace."

I could not face this figure, kept my eyes
on Virgil's heels, following close behind.
As the soft breeze in May before the dawn

feels with its scent of dew-wet grass and flowers
I felt a wing brush my brow, heard these words:
"Blessèd are those without foul appetite

whose only hunger is for what is right."

25: To the Lustful

1 The time had come to climb without delay
for it was after noon. The narrow way
made us go single file. Within my brain

4 a question formed. Just like a little stork
wishing to fly, raises a wing, but since
it fears to leave the nest, drops it again,

7 I was like that, hardly dared clear my throat
when without backward glance my master spoke:
"You are on fire to ask me something. Shoot!"

10 Assured once more I said, "Shades do not eat,
so what makes some of them so very thin?"
Said he, "Our figures in a looking glass

13 are bodiless, yet show us as we are,
thinner or fatter though they do not eat.
I know a better explanation's due.

16 Statius, may I pass that job to you?"
Came the reply, "You know as much as I,
but your request is one that I accept."

19 Statius told me, "Listen son, and learn.
The human male's creative fluids go
through vein and heart, infuse and shape each part

until in loving acts they overflow
the female vessel, thus fertilising
her passive fluids into a new life

with whole new soul, but not yet rational.
Think it a plant containing seeds. These sprout
into organs that it needs, moving like

water creature, jellyfish or tadpole
stirring in the womb. By natural growth
these turn into a complex animal.

How animal becomes a child with mind
is mystery. A wiser man than we,
Arabian Averroes, could find

no organ of self-consciousness so said
it naturally grew in new-born brains.
Untrue! Believe what Aquinas deduced.

As soon as nature forms the foetal brain
the First Creator welcomes it as His.
Rejoicing, he breathes into it His own

freedom that can reflect upon itself.
Think of how sunlight changes grapes to wine.
God's gift of free thought is far more divine.

When, after life, the soul is loosed from flesh
it keeps those faculties it gained in life –
memory, intelligence and will –

but more enhanced, much keener than before.
These rush it to the one or other shore
where wait the ferries that will take them to

49 fit states in Hell or here, for what they've made
of their immortal souls now radiate
on air their shapes and size while still alive,

52 as sunbeams build across a rain-wet sky
a bow of colours to entrance the eye.
That shape moves as the soul moves, for each sense

55 has organs letting it walk, speak, smile, weep
as you experienced. Passions change
souls, shapes, as appeared in glutton's ring,

58 prompting you to ask for explanation."
We set foot on the last road round that height,
turned right and I was terrified to see

61 huge flames that blasted from the inner cliff
to almost reach the ring-road's outer edge.
A strong up-draft of wind from down below

64 drove back that fiery hedge a little way,
leaving space along the precipice's edge
where we could walk in single file, me last

67 between cremation and a deadly fall.
My master said (but did not need to say)
"Be careful here and do not swerve at all."

70 Then from the endless bonfire at my side
that mighty hymn, *O Lord have mercy* came,
sung by a band of spirits in the flame.

73 Fear for my skin and curiosity
made me stare to and fro between my feet
and choir of shades who, finishing the hymn

then cried aloud the words that Mary said
on hearing she was carrying a child:
But I have never known a man! They then

softly began singing the hymn again.
After each hymn they chanted a new phrase
denouncing lust or praising chastity,

and with these penances they pass their days.

26: The Lustful

1 While my good master still called out to me,
"Take care! Beware!" we walked in single file
along the precipice's outer rim.

4 The sinking sun made bright the Western sky
and being at our altitude it cast
my shadow on the flames we travelled past,

7 so yellow flames appeared to burn more red.
As all the shades were journeying our way
the nearest ones attended to that sight.

10 A pair on whom I eavesdropped near me said,
"That man lives in the flesh." "Yes, I agree,"
whereupon both came close to me although

13 carefully keeping in the fire because
escaping it was not their main desire.
One questioned me, "O you who walk behind

16 the other two, tell me (burning with thirst
in dreadful heat) what others want to know.
How come you here without having to die?"

19 A strange sight silenced me before I spoke.
From far ahead I saw a running crowd
come down that blazing road, and rushing past

they kissed the crowd advancing on my side
so fast that no delay was caused, like ants
exchanging nose-rubs to convey good will.

Not stopping all tried to out-shout the rest.
"Sodom! Gomorrah!" those departing yelled.
Those going my way bawled, "The Cretan queen

in wooden cow got fucked by bull!"
As cranes divide, one flight departing north
to Arctic snows, one south to Egypt's sands,

both sides went different ways, singing hymns,
chanting scripture, with tears confessing sins,
and thus in pain obtaining holiness.

Those who had first approached me came again,
and I, respecting their desire began,
"O souls whose thirst for righteousness will be

as Jesus said, fulfilled at last one day,
in Paradise a saint has ordered me
to look at what God made for humankind

from the world's centre to the outmost stars.
But say (for I will write it in a book)
who were those folk going the other way?

And also, who are you?" The couple gaped
like Highlanders bemused by city streets
but soon resumed civility again.

The first shade said, "Your soul is truly blest.
It will learn how to die better than most.
Those you saw run the other way have sinned

as Caesar did, whose soldiers called him 'queen'.
They shout 'Sodom' in self-reproach. We too
enjoyed unlawful feasts of lust. My crowd

shout the disgraceful name of Pasiphaë
who in lust turned into beast. I do not know
all who are here. Guido Guinicelli

is my name. I so sorrowed for my sins
death sent me quickly here. I'll soon be free."
In King Lycurgus' time two orphan boys

found that their mother lived. I partly felt
their joy on hearing Guido's name for he
wrote best the earliest Italian verse,

in sweet and graceful songs of love. I gazed
speechlessly 'til, after my sight was fed,
I offered my respect in humble words

he could not doubt, and said, "Thank you but why
with words and looks you value me so high,
I cannot think." Said I, "Your noble verse

in common speech of shop and street enrich
our talk and thought. Thus, sacred is the ink
you wrote them in." "Brother," said he, "look there!"

He pointed to a shade ahead. "In verse
and prose romance he had more craftsmanship.
Fools deny this, misguided by the cry

of other fools who set mere fashion high
above good rules of reason and of art.
Let me be selfish, if you will be kind.

When you ascend to Paradise and find 76
that monastery where the abbot is
our Lord Christ Jesus, there please pray for me.

He sank back into flames like fish in sea. 79

27: Chastity

1 Midnight in Spain; high noon in Asia;
sun nearing dawn at Calvary where Christ
was crucified; here, ready to depart.

4 Upon the cliff edge, close beside the flames,
God's happy angel welcomed us and sang
in voice more clear than any I had heard,

7 "Blest are the pure in heart! Come, holy souls,
pass through this fire and climb to Paradise!"
His last words struck me with a deathly chill.

10 I have seen people burned alive. Raising
clasped hands I glared into the flame. Virgil
turned to me, said, "Son, here is agony

13 but certainly not death. Recall, recall
our ride on Geryon. I brought us through!
I'll do the same now we are nearer God.

16 If you were in this flame a thousand years
it would not burn a hair upon your head.
Go closer if you fear I'm fooling you.

19 Test it with your garment hem. Put away,
put away fear! Enter with confidence!"
But still I stood, in spite of conscience.

My fearful stubbornness now troubled him.
"Remember that this fiery wall," he said,
"divides from Beatrice." Hearing that name

I softened, stared at him. "So now we go?"
he murmered, with a smile as at a child
beguiled with promise of a sweet. He then

told Statius to come behind me and
strode first into the fire. On entering
I felt a bath in molten glass would be

a cooling change, so terrible the pain,
but my sweet father spoke of Beatrice
to lead me on: "I seem to see her eyes,

rejoice!" he said. A new voice led me too,
singing, "Come you whom God the Father blest!"
Once again I came out into a light

too bright for me to see. Now the voice said,
"Evening has come. Don't stop. Start up the stair
before the west grows dark." Straight through the rock

the narrow staircase went, with sun so low
my shadow filled it up ahead. Night fell.
That hill lets none go forward after dark.

Each sank to make his bed upon a step
as goats in morning light that leap at play
in noonday heat rest, chewing cud in shade,

watched by the goatherd leaning on his staff –
as shepherds also watch their flocks by night,
ensuring no wild beast attempts a raid,

I, like a goat between two herdsmen, lay
in that high-walled ravine where I could see
only a few stars overhead, but these

were bigger, brighter than I'd ever seen,
and as I gazed sleep seized me, sleep that brings
sometimes good news of things to come. Venus,

our morning star, had risen from the sea
I think, and cast a ray upon the hill
when I dreamed that a lady came to me,

beautiful and young, through level meadows
gathering spring flowers. She also sang,
"Know, if you want my name, that I am Leah,

and weave these garlands to adorn myself,
unlike my sister Rachel who all day
sits before her mirror, loving her eyes,

while I adore the garments that I weave."
And now the dawn in splendour touched the sky.
Shadows fled everywhere and so did sleep.

The poets had arisen. So did I.
"The fruit that mortals seek on many trees,
you will pluck today," I heard Virgil say.

No promise ever pleased as much. Each step
made me feel wings were sprouting on my heels.
Reaching the top he looked at me and said,

"You've seen the Hellish, also purging fires.
I've led you by intelligence and skill
up to this level where I have no power.

From here, let happiness decide your way.
see how the sunlight glows on you and on
smooth grassy lawn, fine trees, fruits and flowers

clothing this gracious soil. The splendid eyes
that chose me as your guide must soon appear.
Rest now or roam as wide as you're inclined.

While Statius and I will follow you.
I am not needed now. Your will is whole,
free, strong. Not to obey it would be wrong.

I crown you king and bishop of your soul."

28: The Earthly Paradise

1 The pleasure of exploring such a wood
by easy strolling over fragrant turf
did my heart good. The green boughs overhead

4 filtered the sunlight into golden gleams.
The sweet air fanned my brows and shook the leaves
around wee tuneful birds whose vocal art

7 cheered me by blending with an undertone
of branches softly murmuring like pines
beside Ravenna when sirocco blows.

10 We strayed so far among these ancient glades
that where we entered them was lost to sight.
Then, just ahead, a stream three paces wide

13 ran past from left to right, grass on each side
wet by small waves. I never saw water
darker and yet so clear. Earth's purest wells

16 are cloudier, though density of shade
prevented sunshine entering, and made
the richly coloured petals of the blooms

19 on the far bank much more astonishing.
A lady plucking them was singing there.
"Lady," I called, "if kindliness belongs

to so majestically fair a face,
come nearer please, to let me hear your songs.
You gather blossoms like Persephone,

dear daughter of the goddess, Mother Earth,
before the King of Hell abducted her,
thus robbing us of spring for half the year."

She turned and danced toward me and her feet
did not depress the crimson and yellow
petals she trod. Erect, at the stream's edge,

still holding this high garden's flowering sprays,
she raised her modest head and smiled at me
with lovely eyes bright as two morning stars.

The strait dividing Asia from Greece
bound both the scope of human pride and love,
from Persia's great king who lost his fleet,

to amorous Leander, whom it drowned.
They loathed the Hellespont. I hated more
that little stream which would not part for me.

"This place, though new to you," the lady said,
"should not feel strange, for it was made by God
exactly to delight the human race.

Adam and Eve first thought it Paradise.
Yet wonder (which I notice on your face)
is natural, for God's creation is

almost too wonderful to understand.
Ask what you wish to know. I will reply."
"Below us on this hill of stairs," said I,

"someone said running streams and moving airs
don't happen here." "They cannot, lower down,"
said she. "This summit is exceptional.

God who delights in generosity
made Adam good, giving him Eve for wife,
this lovely, perfect garden for their home

raised far above the stormy seas and lands
of Earth and Hell where Satan is interred.
Here they enjoyed both peaceful ease and mirth,

where all good kinds of tree, herb, fruit and bloom
flourish abundantly. By sin they lost
this best, first human nest, exchanging it

for grief, pain, toil in nations you know well.
From these their children graduate to Hell
or rise to Paradise by climbing here.

Though clouds are lifted upward by the sun,
the triple steps of penitence exist
so high that nothing misty reaches them,

so no one being purified by pain
is hurt by harsher natures than their own.
Air stirring tree tops gently at this height

circles the globe, as the First Mover wills
who turns the bodies of celestial light –
the moon, sun, planets and constellations.

Thus, seeds from here are carried by the air
world-wide to all the nations, taking root
in soil that suits them best. No rain falls here

so far above the clouds. A fountain fed
by God's will flows out in two steady streams.
This we call Lethe, the other Eunoë.

Who drink this lose all memory of sin;
the next renews all memory of good.
Drunk later, it has sweetest taste of all.

Soon these will quench your thirst, but first of all
you may welcome news I'd like to add.
Ancient poets spoke of a Golden Age

when all was good and nothing went amiss.
Here is the former homeland of their dreams.
Nectar they sang about was in these streams."

My fellow poets smiled, nodded at this.

29: Revelation

1 She sang like one in love, "blessèd are they
whose sins are purified". Like woodland nymph
seeking or shunning shade among the trees

4 she walked upstream, and on the other side
I also walked, fitting my steps to hers.
Less than a hundred paces further on

7 the banks curved equally in such a way
we both faced east again. She called to me,
"Look, brother – listen!" for upon us dawned

10 far greater brightness through each branch and leaf,
and with it such sweet melody rang out
I blamed Eve for her eating of that fruit

13 which stopped me knowing such delights before.
So on I went, experiencing joys
that grew as brightness grew, while melody

16 became a hymnal and triumphant choir.
O holy virgins who inspire all art,
if sleepless toil and pain and poverty

19 have been my part in seeking for your aid,
I beg from all of you again, but most
Urania, muse of celestial things,

to fix in verse thoughts difficult to think.
On the far brink ahead I seemed to see
the golden trunks of seven stately trees,

but as I neared their place, saw them to be
majestic candlesticks, linked at the base.
As voices sang hosannas each one flamed

bright as midsummer moons. Awestruck, I gazed
at Virgil who looked back, just as amazed.
Staring again on these high things, I saw

their stems approach slow as a new-made bride
down a cathedral aisle. The lady said,
"Why love big lights more than their followers?"

I saw behind men clad in purer white
than seen on Earth. I paused and saw the stream
reflect my left side mirror-like. Above

I saw each flame staining the air behind
with the bright colours sunshine paints through rain,
which left a rainbow flag or canopy

ten paces wide, whose end I could not see.
Twenty-four elders walked in pairs beneath.
With wreaths of lilies on their heads they sang,

"Hail, loveliest of Adam's daughters who
in paradise is now divinely blessed."
They passed, and flowers filled the further bank

while brightness grew as four great beasts arrived,
crowned with green leaves and having six wings each,
wings spotted with gold eyes like peacocks' tails,

but these were watchful eyes. Ezekiel
in the Old Testament tells how these came
from freezing cold through cloud, storm, flame, with more

of how they look than I have time, reader,
to tell in rhyme. He says they have four wings.
Saint John's *Apocalypse* agrees with me.

Between the beasts a chariot, two-wheeled,
moved on behind a griffin with two wings
raised high beyond my sight. They neatly clasped

the central green band of the canopy,
nor cut the three bright colours on each side.
The griffin's eagle-half was all of gold,

the lion-half pure white with mingled red.
Rome never gladdened hero-emperors
with such a car, more vivid than the sun

when Phaeton plunged its horses down the sky.
Three nymphs danced in a ring by the right wheel.
One glowed so vivid red that in a fire

she'd be invisible. The second seemed
all emerald, the third like fallen snow.
Red and white led the dance alternately,

but red sang, and according to her voice
she and the other two moved fast or slow.
At the left wheel four nymphs in purple dress

also rejoiced in dancing, and were led
by she who had three eyes within her head.
Behind these groups appeared two ancient men

in gravity and dignity alike
but differently clad. One wore the garb
of he whose kindly art can heal the sick –

Hippocrates. One seemed the opposite,
holding a sword so sharp, bright, threatening
I shuddered, though between him and me

flowed the deep stream. Four elders followed these
with humble looks, and last of all came one
whose face was keen, though walking in his sleep.

The garments of these seven final men
were white, like the first twelve. Their brows were crowned,
not with white lilies, but with rosy wreaths

so red their heads all seemed to be aflame.
The car came opposite me and stopped
with thunderclap that halted all the rest.

The rainbow flag above them ceased to flap.

30: Beatrice

Just as at night the seven stars we call
The Plough and Charlie's Wain and The Great Bear
guide all good steersmen on the salt sea plain,

so three great Christian virtues: Faith, Hope, Love,
with Courage, Wisdom, Justice, Temperance
(four virtues Pagans recognise) create

to eyes not blinded by the fog of sin,
the candelabrum holding seven flames
which light for us the way to God above.

The Heavenly Grace I know as Beatrice
is carried by His chariot, the Kirk
whose baring pole is the true cross of Christ.

After it halted, all the twenty-four
pure white-robed, leaf-crowned patriarchs between
candles and griffin turned toward the car

with smiling faces, blissfully serene,
and one inspired by Heaven, sang three times,
O come to me from Lebanon, my bride.

The others joined their melody to his
like blessèd souls on Resurrection Day,
raised by the clang of the last trump to sing

hosannas with rejuvenated tongue.
At the great sound I saw above the car
a hundred angel ministers appear

who sang, *Blessèd is she who comes*, and then,
O give her lilies with full hands. They flung
up and around flowers of every kind.

I once saw in the dawning of a day
a rosy eastern sky, clear blue above,
while low white mist so gently veiled the sun,

my eyes could linger on its perfect sphere.
Thus in the cloud of blooms from angel hands
that whirled and fell inside the car and out,

a lady came, with olive garland crowned
and white veil, misting a green dress through which
her loveliness shone like a living flame.

I had not felt the awe now filling me
for many years. I had first felt it when
a child of nine, I met another child

I loved unselfishly, and so knew then
what press of adult care made me forget –
that love can be and ought to be divine.

The goddess now reminded me of this.
I turned to Virgil in my sore distress
as a child turns to mother in a fright

meaning to say, "I tremble with despair –
how can I make my treachery come right?"
He was not there. Virgil, my dearest friend,

49 the good guide who had led me safe through Hell,
and washed my cheeks with dew to make me fit
to climb so close to my salvation

52 had vanished. Gone. I wept, then heard a voice.
"Don't weep now, Dante. You must shed more tears
for worse than loss of Virgil's company."

55 Hearing my name I turned and saw her stand
within the car, speaking across the stream
as admirals commanding fleets address

58 a sailor, from a flagship's highest deck.
The veil descending from her head, held there
by olive-wreath-sprays from Minerva's tree

61 did not allow a clear view of her face,
and yet the regal way she spoke conveyed
her harshness was restrained by tenderness.

64 "Look well at me. I am your Beatrice.
How dare you weep up here? Did you not know
this paradise is made for happiness?"

67 Ashamed, I stared down into the pure stream;
saw my glum face reflected; turned away.
Stern pity has for me a bitter taste.

70 She spoke no further as the angels sang
the psalm that starts, *My hope is in the Lord*,
ending with, *You give freedom to my feet.*

73 They seemed to say, *Lady, why blame him so?*
Such Heavenly compassion warmed and thawed
ice that had bound my heart. This flowed away

like candlewax in flame, or frozen snow
packed hard by northern blasts between the firs
upon the Apennines (Italy's spine)

melting in breezes out of Africa.
I who had never so profoundly grieved,
poured from my eyes and mouth, water and sighs.

They proved my agony was honesty.
Still upright in her car my lady said,
"You spirits living in eternal day

know well why he's to blame. I only asked
to let him hear me make his falseness plain.
Repentance needs his grief to equal guilt,

sorrow to balance his dead weight of sin.
The starry wheels that turn the universe
let folk bring gifts from God to splendid ends,

but only through their will. He had great gifts.
With care they would have yielded splendid fruit,
yet in good soil foul weeds may also sprout.

Our childhood love preserved his innocence.
His adolescence brought new friends, but sight
of my young eyes at times still kept him right.

When twenty-five I died and was reborn
in purity, while his acquaintances
misled his will, because he now pursued

visions of good that could not be made real.
In dreams and memories I called him back.
He did not heed, sank low till Heaven feared

103 for his salvation. Only showing him
the wholly lost in Hell could save his soul;
and so I went to Limbo, found the man

106 who led him here where I will be his guide,
for I must lead him to a greater height
that poetry may show to folk on Earth

109 the architecture of eternity.
But Heaven would undo its high decrees
were he not first washed clean in Lethe's stream.

112 The saltest tears must pay his entrance fees."

31: The Cleansing

"You on the far side of this sacred stream –" 1
(she thrust this sharp point of her speech at me)
"have heard my accusation. Is it true?"

Such weakness and confusion mastered me 4
I struggled for a word but none would come.
She let me stand there dumb a while, then said,

"Reply. Say what you think. Bad memories 7
have not yet been destroyed by Lethe's drink."
Fear piercing my confusion forced a "Yes"

so faint only her eyes could know I spoke. 10
I stood like a poor archer whose bow broke
letting the arrow go, so it fell short.

Under such fierce assault more tears and sobs 13
were now my sole resort. Again she spoke.
"When love of me led you to love good things

beyond which nothing better can be found, 16
what road blocks, spike-topped fences or deep moats
stopped you from going onward as you should?

What tempted you to leave the path of good?" 19
My lips had trouble shaping a reply
but after a deep sigh I stammered this.

22 "When I lost hope of seeing you again
domestic life and local politics
seemed adequate distractions from my pain,

25 with some erotic dissipation too."
Said she, "If you had tried to justify
facts you have just declared and this court knows,

28 and done that shamelessly with a dry face,
my condemnation would increase your woes.
Not so. To bear the shame of your offence

31 will help resist all future siren calls.
Stop weeping now. Hear what you should have learned
from my dead body. Yes, nature and art

34 had never shown such beauty as was mine
which crumbled into dust. Since death stole that,
why dally with more bodies that must die?

37 I went to Heaven. You should have prepared
to join me here where death does not exist,
and let no other women hold you back

40 where all death-strokes must fall." With downcast head
I stood, my guilt confessed, reproved. She said,
"Since hearing gives you grief, look up for more.

43 Come, elevate your beard." No wind tore up
tough oak tree by its roots slower than I
lifted my rough chin at her mocking words.

46 Angels had stopped casting their cloud of blooms.
Beatrice stood gazing with enraptured face
upon the creature harnessed to her car –

the griffin with two natures in one soul.
Beyond the Lethe stream, beneath her veil
she was more beautiful than when on Earth

her face had been the loveliest of all.
The nettle of remorse so stung me that
hatred of all I ever liked but she,

with such self-loathing, cut into my heart
I lost idea of self and time and place.
When heart at last restored some gleam of sense

the lady first encountered in the wood
was saying, "Hold on! Don't let go my hand."
I lay throat deep in Lethe's cleansing stream,

but floating and upheld by one so light,
she walked upon the stream, her arm so strong
her hand was firmly pulling me along.

Near the far bank in words I can't recall
she sang about forgiveness, held my head,
plunged it beneath the stream, and so I drank,

then free of guilt at last could step ashore.
The four nymphs by the nearest chariot wheel
raised arms and linked their hands above my head.

"In Heaven we appear as stars," they said,
"and before Beatrice arrived on Earth
were chosen as her serving maidens here.

Now we will lead you round to see her eyes,
but fully to enjoy the light in them
hear the three dancers by the other wheel

76 who see more deeply into them than we."
Led there, I stood before the griffin's breast,
staring at Beatrice in the car behind.

79 Her serving maids then sang in unison,
"Now you will see the eyes of emerald
which pierced you with love's dart. Don't fear to gaze."

82 Since the veil did not hide her eyes I stared
and saw within their depth the two-fold beast
like sun's reflection in a looking glass.

85 Reader, this wonderful and lovely sight –
this figure changing in my lover's eyes,
now with a Heavenly aspect, now the Earth's,

88 was nourishing, like a delicious meal
that never would reduce true appetite.
Then the three virtues from the other wheel,

91 Faith, Hope and Love, danced around me and sang,
"O Beatrice, unveil your lovely face,
to gratify this faithful traveller

94 who's journeyed more than any man alive,
down through the world and up to this great height
to look upon the glory of your Grace!"

97 Though drunk with language's magnificence
what poet, pale from studying his art
won't find himself unable to impart

100 the greatest thing made present to his sense?

32: Of the Kirk

Her lovely smile was all I wished to see. 1
For ten years I had thirsted for the sight.
I fixed my eyes on her and in delight

forgot all else but she. Again the net 4
of her enchantment was surrounding me
until I heard the Virtues call, “Too fixed!”

when this recalled me from my dazzled state. 7
I found the sacred pageant had swung round.
Candles and prophets now marched to the sun,

passing the car just as the griffin turned 10
into the new course with an easy force
that stirred no feather of its wings. I walked

with she who’d ferried me and Statius. 13
Beside the car we crossed the woodland glades
lost to mankind because the serpent’s tongue

had misled Eve. Three arrow flights beyond 16
our turning point the car stopped at a tree
far loftier than any I had seen.

Leafless and blossomless, the branches spread 19
wider while rising to astounding height.
Murmuring, “Adam’s tree”, our company

22 encircled it as Beatrice left the car.
The rest sang, "Hail, Griffin who ate no fruit
from this forbidden tree, thus saving seed

25 of righteousness from those who find it sweet
until its poison makes their bellies squirm."
The griffin drew the car to the tree trunk,

28 laid the pole on a branch, and as in spring
the plants renew themselves, so did the tree.
Its colour flushed through rose to violet.

31 It put forth buds, unfolded leaves and bloom
as a glad hymn was sung, but not by me
who fell asleep. Artists perhaps may paint

34 how I looked then. I can't, so pass to when
light entered eyes and someone said, "Arise",
the word Christ used to wake dead Lazarus.

37 My good guide through the stream was at my side.
I asked, "Where's Beatrice?" and she replied,
"Sitting beside the car on the tree root,

40 shaded by leaves. Around her like a cloister
the Virtues stand, candle in hand, each one
guarding a flame. The griffin is again

43 with prophets, saints, angels in paradise."
She may have said much more but Beatrice
was all I noticed now, on the bare ground,

46 her seven hand-maids near. She spoke to me.
"Now for a while become a woodlander
and citizen of Rome as Rome should be

when Christ is Roman too. Here and elsewhere
remember all you see. When back on Earth
write of it truthfully. Do the world good."

I saw Jove's eagle swoop down through the tree,
beak tearing leaves, the blossoms and smooth bark.
It struck the car, rocking it side to side,

to and fro like a boat in stormy tide.
Then there leapt in a filthy starving fox!
Rebuked by Beatrice the vile thing fled.

The eagle now nested within the car,
feathering it with golden plumes until
from on high I heard a lamenting cry,

"My wee car, O how you are weighted down!"
Then I saw ground between wheels opening
letting a dragon out that drove its tail

through the car floor. Like wasp removing sting
it pulled tail out and wandering away
left the poor broken car encased in plumes,

thick as knot-grasses clogging fertile soil.
No doubt the donors of the plumes meant well,
but the transforming chariot grew heads.

Along the shaft were three with oxen horns.
At the car corners grew another four,
each with a single horn upon its brow.

This monster never seen on Earth before
had riding on its back a naked whore
gazing triumphantly around as if

76 a conqueror upon a citadel,
while at her side a shameless giant stood
kissing, caressing her until he saw

79 her amorously try to catch my eye.
Beating her viciously from head to toe,
he dragged away both her and that foul steed

82 till both were hidden by the leafy wood.

33: The Final Cleansing

"O God, see heathens in your holy places!"
The seven Virtues chanted through their tears,
first three, then four, joining this psalm of loss.

They paused when Beatrice, with such a sigh
as Mary must have sighed at foot of cross
stood up and glowing like a flame, proclaimed,

"Dear sisters, we must leave here for a while
but will return." A gesture made them walk
ahead of her, while we three came behind

until she turned her calm clear eyes on me
saying, "Come nearer, brother. We must talk.
Ask what you wish." I was so far beneath

her holy state, my tongue tripped on my teeth
in stammering reply: "My la-la-la-
my la-la-lady knows what I should know

mu-much, much more than me." "Then start," said she,
"by talking sensibly, and not like one
stumbling under a load of sin. Lethe

has washed you clean. You saw the vile dragon
breaking my car, a giant drag it off.
Know those to blame will not escape God's wrath.

22 Know that the eagle feathering my car,
making it monstrous, then slave to a hag,
will not forever have heirs acting so.

25 The birthday of a hero, sent by God
to kill the giant and his prostitute
is registered on the star calendar.

28 Exactly when and where I do not know.
Five hundred, ten and five are numbers where
some find a clue. Not me. Such prophecies

31 like Sphinx's riddle, hide what should be plain,
yet when on Earth again tell it to those
who race to death, because it will come true.

34 Write of the tree: what you saw, what I say.
It is the tallest tree, widest at top
because God made it only for himself.

37 Adam learned robbing it is blasphemous,
dwelling with Eve in Hell five thousand years
till Jesus let him out. The latest theft

40 which you have seen is recent history.
But now I fear your mind is like a stone
so darkened that my words must dazzle you.

43 Remember them, though you don't understand."
Said I, "As sealing wax receives its stamp
I am impressed by you and all you say,

46 but why do words you utter fly so high
over my head? The more I try (alas!)
the less I know." "Which teaches you," she said,

"your knowledge is as far below my own
as Earth is underneath a Heavenly Star."
I cried, "But I have never left your side!"

She smiled and said, "You have drunk Lethe, so
forget how many years you walked astray.
Now you must suffer more to understand."

The splendid sun stood at the height of noon
(which varies with a viewer's latitude)
when the seven maids who had gone ahead

paused on the strand of what at first I thought
a waterfall shaded by mountain trees.
Nearer I saw an overflowing spring

diverging in two streams as different
as Tigris and Euphrates are, but yet
they parted as reluctantly as friends.

"O light and glory of the human race,
what are these waters?" I asked Beatrice,
who said, "Matilda knows." My other guide

quickly replied like one discarding blame,
"I've told him both these rivers' name and use."
"His memory is numbed," said Beatrice,

"by novelties, but here flows Eunoë.
As you know how, refresh his weakened mind."
Gentle souls gladly serve another's will.

Matilda murmured, "Come." She took my hand,
saying to Statius, "and you come too."
Reader, if I had time to write of it,

76 I'd speak about the sweetness of the stream
I tasted then. I thirst to drink it still
but now must fill more pages with the tale

79 of my long poem's third, last, greatest part.
Commanded by the art I can't deny.
I leave the stream of Eunoë renewed,

82 a clean soul entering the starry sky.